LET'S NOT KEEP FIGHTING THE TROJAN WAR

## Among Edward Sanders Books

Poem from Jail (1963)

Peace Eye (1966)

The Family: The Manson Group and Aftermath (1971, Updates 1990, 2002)

Egyptian Hieroglyphics (1973)

Tales of Beatnik Glory, Volume I (1975)

Investigative Poetry (1976)

20,000 A.D. (1976)

Fame & Love in New York (1980)

The Z-D Generation (1981)

Thirsting for Peace in a Raging Century: Selected Poems 1961–1985 (1987)
New and Revised Edition (2009)

Tales of Beatnik Glory, Volumes 1 & 2 (1990)

Hymn to the Rebel Cafe—Poems 1986-1991 (1993)

Chekhov: A Biography in Verse (1995)

1968: A History in Verse (1997)

The Poetry and Life of Allen Ginsberg (2000)

America: A History in Verse: Volume 1. 1900-1939 (2000)

Volume 2. 1940-1961 (2000)

Volume 3. 1962-1970 (2004)

Tales of Beatnik Glory Vols. 1–4 (2004)

Poems for New Orleans (2008)

America, a History in Verse, the Twentieth Century, CD edition (2009)

## Recent Chapbooks

Stanzas for Social Change (2005)

This Morning's Joy (2008)

Revs of the Morrow (2008)

## CDs

Sanders Truckstop (1970)

Beer Cans on the Moon (1972)

Songs in Ancient Greek (1988)

American Bard (1995)

Thirsting for Peace (2005)

Poems for New Orleans (with Mark Bingham) (2007)

# LET'S NOT KEEP FIGHTING THE TROJAN WAR

NEW AND SELECTED POEMS 1986–2009

## Edward Sanders

COFFEE HOUSE PRESS : : MINNEAPOLIS : : 2009

Coffee House Press books are available to the trade through our primary distributor, Consortium Book Sales & Distribution, www.cbsd.com. For personal orders, catalogs, or other information, write to: Coffee House Press, 79 Thirteenth Avenue NE, Suite 110, Minneapolis, MN 55413.

Coffee House Press is a nonprofit literary publishing house. Support from private foundations, corporate giving programs, government programs, and generous individuals helps make the publication of our books possible. We gratefully acknowledge their support in detail in the back of this book.

Good books are brewing at coffeehousepress.org

LIBRARY OF CONGRESS CATALOGING-IN-PUBLICATION DATA

Sanders, Ed.

Let's not keep fighting the Trojan war : selected poems, 1986–2008 /
by Edward Sanders ; introduction by Joanne Kyger.

p. cm.

ISBN 978-1-56689-234-6 (alk. paper)

I. Title.

PS3569.A49L48 2009

811'.54--dc22

2009022843

PRINTED IN THE UNITED STATES

10 9 8 7 6 5 4 3 2 1

FIRST EDITION | FIRST PRINTING

ACKNOWLEDGMENTS: Some of the poems in this book were published in the following magazines: *Woodstock Journal, Beat Scene, The World, Sulfur, Scarlet, Café Review, Home Planet News, House Organ, Hanging Loose, Vanitas, Heartland, Intent, San Francisco Magazine, Scarlet, La Selva Subterranea, River Styx, UpRiver/DownRiver, So Nice to See You, Long Shot, Mechachabe, Notus. atelier 2, Food and Water Journal,* and *Taos Review.*

The poem tracing Anton Chekhov's final minutes appeared in the anthology, *Literature and its Writers, an Introduction to Fiction, Poetry, and Drama* (Bedford Books).

Some of these poems appeared in the following books: *Hymn to the Rebel Café* (Black Sparrow), *Stanzas For Social Change* (Shivastan), *This Morning's Joy* (Limberlost Press), *The Poetry & Life Of Allen Ginsberg* (Overlook Press), *America, A History In Verse, Vol. 2* (1940–1961) (Black Sparrow), *Revs Of The Morrow* (Vanitas), *Cracks Of Grace* (Woodland Pattern).

If any of these poems appeared in publications whose names have not been preserved by the author during these energetic decades, he apologizes.

*For Miriam, who made it possible,
and to the memory of my early teacher Lecie Hall,
and to Professor Bluma Trell at* NYU
*who opened up the beauty of Greek lyric poetry*

## Ginsberg

## Aeschylus

## Poetics

## The Long Voyage Home

## The View of Centuries

# Introduction

Ed Sanders doesn't really need an introduction. He is well known, "famous," in the lineage of American Poetry. But if this new and selected is your first reading of his work, you will be introduced to a poet, novelist, journalist, musician, songwriter, performer, scholar, philosopher, publisher, environmentalist, pacifist, and a sincere radical. "I'm idealistic enough to believe that you have to have ideals and you have to work for them. While I breathe, I hope." *

Born in Kansas City, Missouri, his education went from the University of Missouri, to jail in New York City (for swimming out to board a Polaris atomic missile submarine in order to persuade the crew to quit), to graduation from New York University with a degree in classics in 1964.

The Peace Eye Bookstore in NYC's Lower East Side, founded by Sanders in 1964, became a center for "poets, madmen, dope freaks, and space cadets." It also housed a museum collection of poets' pubic hairs, Allen Ginsberg's jar of vaseline, and provided space to edit and publish his magazine, *Fuck You, A Magazine of the Arts,* a scholarly endeavor that reflected the language and style of the time—post-Beat and early-hippie.

His band, The Fugs—formed with Tuli Kupferberg in early 1965—also practiced at The Peace Eye, adding to the intensity of the place. His satiric lyrics about sex, drugs, and politics caused outraged responses from some. To others, however, song titles like "River of Shit," "Whimpers from the Jello," "Group Grope" and "Ramses II Is Dead, My Love," showed a refreshing new direction in the possibilities of song lyrics.

I first saw Ed Sanders during the unique Berkeley Poetry Conference, which took place during two weeks in July of 1965. One of the watershed events in the world of poetry, the conference brought together representatives of American poetry as outlined and published by editor Donald M. Allen in his groundbreaking anthology, *The New American Poetry: 1945–1960.*

As one of the seven poets to give a lecture at this event, Jack Spicer, in what was the last public event of his life, spoke on poetry

---

* *Paste Magazine* interview with Matt Fink.

and politics. The title of Sanders's new and selected responds to this event, forty-four years later. Jack Spicer, in his play *Trolius*, quotes Zeus as saying: "The Trojan War has been going on for the last 3000 years and it hasn't stopped yet. All the stories you've heard about the destruction of Troy are just daydreams Ulysses invented to keep himself sane. You've probably dreamed like that yourselves, waiting for a war to come to an end . . . The people in the play don't seem to know how long the war has lasted . . . Human beings don't have a very good time sense."

Ed Sanders read his poetry a few days later on July 17 during a special reading with John Sinclair, Ted Berrigan, and Lenore Kandel. Allen Ginsberg introduced the group. Ed was entirely distinctive and confident on stage. He didn't merely "read" his poems, he gave a whole other direction to his performance. He was like a young medicine man entering the ranks of *The New American Poetry*. He was, as he remains to this day, able to be on the stage or on the page with the same startling intensity and energy.

A few evenings later he was providing support to the behemoth-like Charles Olson during his authoritative and somewhat fractured free-form lecture, Causal Mythology. "I'm with you boss!" Sanders shouted from the audience—which, after two hours, was beginning to abandon the auditorium. His affection for this great figure, Charles Olson, whom he first read in 1960, is presented in this volume, with lively incidents of recollection. Sanders refers to him as "always on stage . . . in a Scholar-Dionysian Lusimelaysian motivity." We follow him through a psilocybin trip with Charles: "Woo look at the elephants! Posdeidon shouted." What a great way to meet your teacher, when he is "showering with blue arcs!"

And although Ed Sanders is well versed in the classic past, re-anchoring Sappho in the present, his writing bypasses the usual channels of conventional writing, offering up a unique psychic and political space. In 1971, he researched and wrote *The Family: The Story of Charles Manson's Dune Buggy Attack Battalion*—a case study of a hippie "family" gone drastically wrong. At one point, reading *The Family* on my sunny front porch, I became so terrified by Ed's description of the killings, I had to stop reading. Then I finally said to myself, these are only words. I can read words. Although I felt as if I was reliving it all.

From there, Sanders stepped into the bardic role of telling history. "Poetry should again assume responsibility for the description of History . . . For poetry to go forward, it has to begin a voyage into the description of historical reality."

Thus he wrote *Investigative Poetry* as a working document for poets, published by City Lights in 1976, inspired by Charles Olson's *Projective Verse* (1950): "A poem is energy transferred from where the poet got it, by way of the poem itself, all the way over to the reader . . . We now enter . . . into the field . . . where all the syllables and all the lines must be managed in their relation to each other."

In Ed's extension of Olson's theme, the page becomes history, filled with data, photos, drawings, and words, free from any particular form of verse or mind. The Complete Bard aims at data, information, history, incident. The poet presents "the spoken text; the text as beauteously presented on the page; and the text as performed."

With this the Investigative Poet, in the bardic tradition, knows how to publicly present poems to bring about the rebirth of the voice, with songs, and the ballad opera. Poetic reality enters into a public presentation of verse—Sanders using his voice like an inspired and confident lark. The ancient image comes alive again with the poet being "he who carries a lyre." Or an electronic necktie.

And here he is with Ted Berrigan in this volume, "slaves to the lyre and the bee." And not getting too well paid for it either. "It's an evil economic system that does not take care of poets." And Sanders does believe in a government that is generous and helps its people. "Everyone has a right to food, a decent place to live, health, & fun." For he is a poet full time— "no weekends for poets." As Ed explains, "a career lasts 60 or 70 years, and a multi-decade research system of proper magnitude and designs can assist in bundles of projects year after year." And Ed has accumulated such projects: *The History of America in Verse in The 20th Century* in five volumes, biographies like *Chekhov,* and *The Poetry and Life of Allen Ginsberg.* Sanders also makes "the news," as participant and observer. His presence in his book *1968* shows him as an active force during the Democratic National Convention in Chicago, hounded by the FBI.

The pieces in this *New and Selected* volume are all open to read with ease and pleasure. Behold, a voice is speaking for our heroes. Rachel Carson, Robert Creeley, Charles Olson, Allen Ginsberg, Ted Berrigan, Sappho, Eric Satie, Lawrence Ferlinghetti, William

Blake, Carl Sandburg . . .

You recall the last
time you saw someone

Or you said goodbye
to an era
a year
a book

The vestiges
remain in the time-track.


Like this book.

—Joanne Kyger

# Waltzing on the Lawn

## A Newly Recovered Poem of Sappho

Rejoice in your beauteous gifts, o youth
and raise high your thrill-toned, love-song lyre!

Once my skin was soft to the touch
but now old age has come to my flesh
and white hair has formed from the dark

Heavy with suffering my soul has been forged
and my knees no longer can bear me up
who used to dance light-leggéd like gamboling fawns

I groan about it thickly   but what can be done?
for no one has the power to be an ageless human

O once the ruby-limbéd Dawn
was smitten with eros
              for Tithonos
and carried him away
to the farthest reaches of the Gaia

But when she begged of Zeus
to make Tithonos immortal
she forgot to ask that
          he be given eternal youth

and so with the passing of time
she kept her fresh-wrought form
while gray old age bewizened her lover

Υ̓́μμες πεδὰ Μοίσαν ἰ]οκ[ό]λπων κάλα δῶρα παῖδες,
σπουδάσδετε καὶ τὰ]ν φιλάοιδον λιγύραν χελύνναν·

ἔμοι δ' ἄπαλον πρίν] ποτ' ἔοντα χρόα γῆρας ἤδη
ἐπέλλαβε, λεῦκαι δ' ἐγ]ένοντο τρίχες ἐκ μελαίναν

βάρυς δέ μ' ὀ [θ]ῦμος πεπόηται, γόνα δ' [ο]ὐ φέροισι,
τὰ δή ποτα λαίψηρ' ἔον ὄρχησθ' ἴσα νεβρίοισι

τὰ <μὲν> στεναχίσδω θαμέως· ἀλλὰ τί κεν ποείην;
ἀγήραον ἄνθρωπον ἔοντ' οὐ δύνατον γένεσθαι

καὶ γάρ π[ο]τα Τίθωνον ἔφαντο βροδόπαχυν Αὔων
ἔρωι φ__α θεῖσαν βάμεν εἰς ἔσχατα γᾶς φέροισα[ν],

ἔοντα [κ]άλον καὶ νέον, ἀλλ' αὖτον ὔμως ἔμαρψε
χρόνωι πόλιον γῆρας, ἔχ[ο]ντ' ἀθανάταν ἄκοιτιν

NOTE: This poem was recently pieced together from two extant papyrus fragments, one at the University of Cologne, and the other among the Oxyrhynchus papyri housed at Oxford University.

The meter is mainly choriambics,

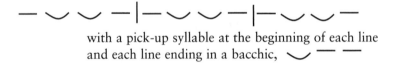

with a pick-up syllable at the beginning of each line and each line ending in a bacchic, ⏑ — —

I have added several lines, not in Sappho's Greek,
which trace for the modern reader the legend of Tithonos &
the deity of the Dawn, Auos. Tithonos was the brother of
Priam, king of Troy, and Auos, daughter of Zeus, was the randy
goddess of the dawn.

# Poetry

Poetry is the shape of eternity
and all equations rest beneath it

Poetry is the rinsing of the sky
& every petal is its form

Verse is the answer to the Question
tell me the truth to "Starry Rhymes"

Poetry is the comet
that traces every crimson couplet

Verse is the cage where
doors stand ever open

Verse is the sky
where wings trace nothing but worded Grace

Poetry is the rolling out
of bloodless drapes on innocent arms

Poetry is Word's way of wanting
& the stone where all waters flow

Poetry is the wending of the wires
for all reciprocated toasts

Verse is the Endall that Ends All

Poetry sings
when doomdreams singe

Poetry is the Full
when people think Empty

Poetry is the faint smell of the grate
where all bread is baked

Poetry is the shape of eternity
and every relation runs under its telling

## The Question of Self-Publishing


For 25 years William Blake
      kept the copper plates for
         the *Songs of Innocence*

to print a copy or two on a need
& then he hand-painted the colors
            with Catherine's help

Walt Whitman helped set & print
         his own *Leaves of Grass*
      in the Brooklyn vastness

Woody Guthrie
a mimeographed edition of his songs in '39

& Ginsberg mimeo'd some "Howl"s
          in '55

& how about Chekhov's *Tales of Melpomene* in 1885
      which he paid for
or Jane Austen's *Sense & Sensibility*
         of 1811?


        *& so it goes*
        *& goes so well*

## Poem for Miriam

She was
    in her
        loose peach gown

'neath a nearly full moon
at midnight

she asked me
to waltz barefoot
        on the lawn

& do th' polka
then lock hands
        & twirl
till the summer stars
           were streaks

I owe her many things
'mong them
    a fresh lesson
        on the power of

*homo ludens*

## Good Time

I'm having a good time tonight
Miriam almost has her painting done
& I'm typing Alf Evers's changes
to part 1 of *Kingston-on-the-Hudson*
while listening to Brahms' Second Symphony
& watching the Nets-Celtics game 5
        with the sound off

## Five Deer

Five deer
lying in the snow
staring at the house


What is this,
a *Star Trek* episode?

## Ferlinghetti

"You know
    what I think?


Fame is
    a disaster"


—Tinker Street, Woodstock, August 23, 2002

## The Impact

It helps to know
there's really nothing to do

That the coyote pack
is howling in the snow

or the generals growling in Baghdad

It's the same as when Mark Twain
was v.p. of the Anti-Imperialist League
in 1903:

"Do not slaughter
at the borders of your power."

But the drive to war
as ancient as the elopement of Helen
stays with our culture
            not that many decades away
            from the slaughter of the Indians

Maybe we can contain it to Gaia
& keep the war cult
            from sluicing
                    into the asteroids

## Scroogosity


Johnson didn't dig
Pope
    translating the *Iliad*
on the backs of letters

—too scroogish
        thought Sam

## September 11

It seemed like such an act of evil
that I was reminded of a postcard
that Manson once sent me

a print of the devil with its long red tongue
dangling down

on which he drew a red swastika

(It was not an upbeat, friendly card)

Miriam and I were publishing
the *Woodstock Journal* at the time

and my friend Austin Metze
designed a cover image

using the M-card devil

A Visit from Hell

# Find Out Who Sartre Is

J. Edgar Hoover
          viewing
an article
in '64
about Jean-Paul Sartre

scrawled
in blue ink
     on its
edge:

          "Find out who
          Sartre is."

# Whispering Books

I know they're not actually talking
but the books on my desk
seem to whisper

—Charles Olson's *Collected Poems*
Blake's *Jerusalem*, E. P. Thompson's
      *The Making of the English Working Class*
even Alfred McCoy's *Politics of Heroin*—
      CIA *Complicity in the Global Drug Trade*
           and others—

"Drop what you're doing!
Set aside your poetry!
Read us! Open us up!
Read **slowly** while you're at it.
**Always** read us
    —every day—
        before you play"

## This Morning's Joy

The half-yearling we call Twist-Foot
hobble-ran across the lawn

Now she can touch her
                mangled right rear hoof
swollen as it is
to the ground

to balance herself
as she eats the corn
we placed on the bluestone

I felt such joy at seeing Twist-Foot
Even a right-wing government
                of hateful war-mongering sleaze
can't knock away
                this morning's joy

**Oh Peace!**

Εἰρήνη

Enter the minds
of men & women

& the minds
of the Milky Way
& Andromeda

if they have any

& when you have made
the Lion-Lamb lie-down

you'd better come up with some food
for sentient beings
o Peace

but please no smoothies
of cosmic dust

# Creeley

## Then Let Them

We were sitting in a college cafeteria
before a reading
and I was feeling down, very down

"You have a lot of friends,"
                    said Bob Creeley

Then he jotted a poem
on a napkin.

## Read, Practice, Play

Creeley
told me how
he was in Rome
a few months ago
& what he most
        hungered
            to do

was stay in his room
& read a biography
        of Wittgenstein!

# Particularity

*Particularity obtains*
*where'er the earth grows green*
*Myself's an echoing ancient frame*
*for all that once was seen*
—Robert Creeley's verse
      for "The New Amazing Grace"

In the springtime
I have learned
            to bring my
            eyes & mind
            ever closer

to the tangled seabed of pain

And, in doing that,
I will face those things
I used to deny,
in fear & boredom,
haste & waste,
till now,
in the raging, tormented,
part-peaceful times—
no more glances, no more glowers
but the abounditude of particularity
                  & the fastnesses of flowers

## A Visit to the Tulip Path

Parked by the Geranium Path
                on Beech Avenue

    Many birds singing
    in Green Fuse energy

    Then up Walnut Avenue
    past

      Fanny Parnell
      1818–1872
      Irish Poet
      & Patriot

A pair of birdwatchers
walk across Fanny's grave
stalking a tall tree

"I like your binoculars,"
                she said
"They're awesome"

    Walnut Avenue is steep
    eyes tear-blinking
    thinking of my own parents
    buried on West Walnut
          at the edge of the prairie

feeling anguish for myself
& the world

guilt for not paying to have the
shrubs on my parents' grave
                    shaped and clipped

guilt for the cowboy boots
Miriam thought I had bought her
on the trip through Placitas
                            in '65

guilt and grief: those trudging twins.


There's a huge European Beech
                    smoky gray and pitted
by the Parker family taphs
at the entrance to the Tulip Path


And then there it is
just as Penelope had said
next to the Creeley family column

with a tall Douglas fir to the back and left

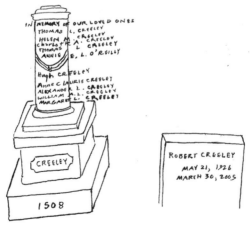

Too upset to sketch a straight line
in this "park of eternal events"

Suffused with others now gone—Olson, Ginsberg
& Sappho

looking down the Tulip Path
toward Robert Creeley

comrade, as if in the time
when that word
had its first glow

I jotted a message

Come on! Creeley!
Swing back out of Marfa!
with some more e-mails
& poems—
please!

and set it by his stone
weeping
pressing my head upon the granite

—May, 21, 2006
Mt. Auburn Cemetery

## Creeley as Therapy


He ran an ad in the health section
                    of the local weekly
"Cure Mental Crises with Creeley."

And you know 12 people
paid $175 for an 8-week workshop!

Enough to put in a new shower stall!

He sat them at ease
                    in a circle of chairs
each of them holding
*The Collected Poems of Robert Creeley 1975–2005*
and then they opened it up at random
read aloud

        & discussed
        the curative feel
                    of the words

as they would relate
to the reader's particular crisis.

It worked!
Smiles cracked the circle
& sometimes tears!

They begged him to hold another one
especially as the calendar
                    tugged toward
                            blue Christmas

# Olson

## Discovering "Maximus from Dogtown—I"


Poe allowed his narrators
to be morose & even bonkers

I think I liked that
when first reading him
around 1953

        Poe
        Whittier
        Frost
        then Pound
        & Ginsberg
        & Dylan Thomas

    my first investigations

Then standing in the 8th St. Bookshop
after class
    in 1960
reading Olson's
    "Maximus from Dogtown— I"

    Wow!

## Olson in Buffalo

'63–'65


He seemed almost in a Hunter Thompson mode
always on stage
in a Scholar-Dionysian
       Lusimelaysian*
          motivity

Buffalo wore him out
    so he wrote a letter of resignation at the airport
        in 1965
but Al Cook allowed the O to remain a professor on leave
till his death over four years later


      Flow thru & past me, O Universe
      for I must say so many No's!

      in order for a string of Yes's
      that could lead to paradise!


*Lusimelaysian: from the Greek word, λυσιμελης, one of Olson's favorite
references, translated as limber-limbed, loose-limbed, or limber-limbic, or
love that "loosens the limbs," as applied to Eros, Love, Passion, Randiness,
and Erotic Fascination.

## Poseidon's Mane

We flew from N.Y. to Boston
on the Eastern Shuttle in the fall of '66
then took a cab to Gloucester

to see the O
in midafternoon
          his morning

Olson had to clear away books
from the stove to make us tea

We had dinner.
Then we were sitting
in the kitchen at Fort Square

We were to stay in the house
rented by Panna Grady
near Dogtown Commons
(she was not there that night)

Olson had a bottle
of orange-red psilocybin pills
& a bottle, literally, of
Acid he'd gotten at Harvard

He went into a back room
& returned with the bottles
of LSD and 'cybin

"Want a swig?" he said
thrusting the liquid acid my direction
as if it were a
shot of rum in a bar by Half Moon Bay.

"A swig!!" I exclaimed

knowing full well that 500 micrograms
was more than enough
why should we risk
some 500,000 microgram
gulps

so we settled on the psilocybin

The O had apparently tried it
in December of 1960 and in February of '61

He spoke later of the
crackerjack quality of the psilo:

"Actually, it's simply a synthetic, about the
size of an old placebo, which
was even smaller than an aspirin, and looks very much
like those fake pills we always were given as though
we needed a cure. . . . In fact when I took it I was
so high on bourbon that I took it like as though
it was a bunch of peanuts. I kept throwing the peanuts
—and the mushroom—into my mouth."
        —from the Gratwick tape, 1963

Olson shook out
a handful of red orange pills

I took about 8
Weaver as I recall had 12

& Olson, at 6 foot 7, had an initial
12 or so, then a few more—

We sat in the kitchen,
and then as the magic mushrooms began to mush

Olson drove us to Dogtown
where we were to sleep

He drove slowly

So slowly that when I looked back behind
a line of cars was close pressed

He pulled over, as I recall
to let some of them roll by,
then we proceeded.

I felt a great surge of confidence
that my mentor, the O, was driving
and he would get us there safely

Then I glanced to the front seat
and Olson had turned into Poseidon!
literally! the Horse from the Sea!
with kelp in his mane
matted and wet

       Of course there is that poem
       in Maximus II
      "All night long
        I was a Eumolpidae
        as I slept
        putting things together
        which had not previously
        fit"

(The Eumolpidae were the descendants of
 Eumolpus, who was a son of Poseidon, and also
 the founder of the Eleusinian Mysteries.
 The Eumolpidae officiated at the Mysteries)

So onward drove Poseidon
—the seat cushions
washed in the froth of his greeny mane
which seemed ornamented with sea wrack,
       bone bits, shells, and oceanic oddments!

I thought, well even if I am bonkers,
the driver, my hero, my guru, my bard
was Safety Assured!

Until we passed a clump of
what appeared to be boulders, in
the gloom to the left.

"Woooo, look at the elephants!"
Poseidon shouted.

We passed a sign

Was it connected with O's lines
"the great ocean is angry
it wants the perfect child"?

We arrived at the stone house
with stone-arched doorway
and sat to talk.

Meanwhile, it seemed as if the place
had become the Chapel Perilous,
and I began to walk outdoors
spend a few minutes
then return back to the Chapel

I did this a few times and
seemed to live through life cycles
as I left the house, walked through the woods
then returned

Once I spoke Akkadian, building a mud brick hut
by the River Euphrates

In another cycle
I was a Hasidic store owner on Hester Street
in the Lower East Side

Weaver later kidded me
        about calling out to the trees

Olson, meanwhile talked onward.
Weaver pointed toward the O:
"Look at those sparks
        coming out of his forehead."

I looked. It seemed
        enormous. This Head-Top
            This Capital

and showering with blue arcs!

On a table was a jade and silver cross
that Dean Stockwell had given John Wieners

I asked the O, "what is there to hold on to?"
He handed me the cross.
I tasted it, and felt it melt in my mouth.

When I went outdoors
Charles warned me about the "quarry"

I recall he was speaking about sachems
and Algonkian longhouses.

Finally, in one of the life cycles
I got lost in the woods

crashing among trees—
leaves in long hair

I must point out that I was
in my full rock and roll attire—
all in red: red boots, red sweater,
red pants, and a red scarf

Finally I threshed down into a street
I thought maybe there had been an accident,

and I was dead

and in fact in Sheol, or purgatory,
                or some kind of Gray Zone.

I walked through deserted Gloucester streets
and was just getting ready to go into a house
                                to get warmer.

Good thing I didn't
A police car came along, and I hailed it

He was at first suspicious of a young man
dressed in red
        with leaves affixed up and down

I recalled Gerrit Lansing's address on Main Street.
Gerrit's friend Derek picked me up at the station
and drove me back to Dogtown

where Olson and Weaver were still talking!
it seemed they had not moved an inch
                        during my adventure!


I called Miriam
        at our pad on Avenue A
and once again, she helped me to land
from another trip into the universal mosaic.

In his first mushroom voyage, Olson
on the Gratwick tape said that he was
"absolutely a peace sachem holding, as chief,
a longhouse ceremony, and I said it in so many words."

        *Oh, Olson! Oh, O!*
*our peace sachem, your forehead aglow*
*in the Dogtown longhouse long ago!*

# Seed Syllables from O

*March 14, 1968*

I had written Charles Olson in Gloucester
for a mantram we could chant in Chicago

I also asked Ed Dorn and d.a. levy.
It came from the chanting the Fugs and the Diggers
had done at the Pentagon (October o' '67)
        "Out, Demons, out! Out, Demons, out!"
and the ceremony with Ginsberg at Senator McCarthy's grave
in early '68

It was worth a try
      to see if a great bard's sung seed syllables
           could help end the war

Olson called Avenue A
      and recited his mantram to Miriam:

    *Plann'd in Creation, Arouse the Nation*
    *Blood is the Food of*
    *Those Gone Mad*
    *Blood is the Food of*
    *Those Gone Mad*
    *Blood is already all over the Nation*
    *Plann'd in Creation, Arouse the Nation*
    *Blood is the Food of*
    *Those Gone Mad*

He then mailed us the Chant
    from Chicago
        on the way to deliver
            his "Poetry & Truth" lectures
                at Beloit College

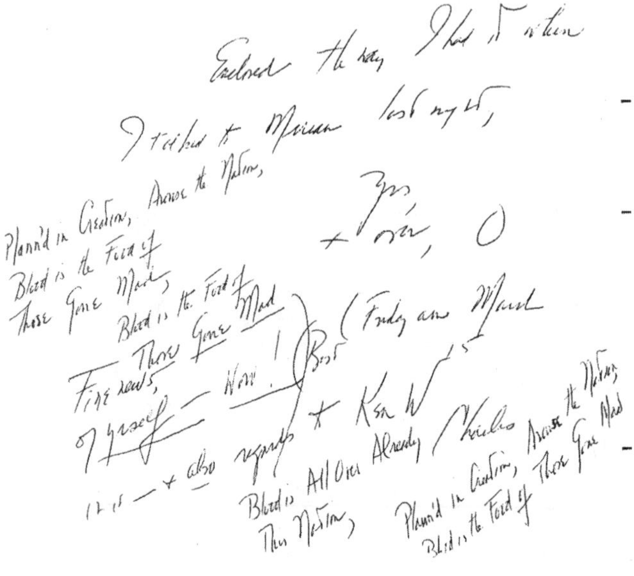


He had his bard-eye
        on a big American problem:
The War Caste wanted blood
                                        (still does)

The evening Olson called &
    chanted his mantram to Miriam
    there was a dinner party, 3 tables of 12,
                                    at Hickory Hill—
    editors and publishers
            from the New York Press Association

At RFK's table sat *Village Voice* writer Jack Newfield
who "argued vigorously for legalization of marijuana
    and shocked the older guests by candidly admitting
    he smoked it himself with some frequency"
                        in the words of
                        one of Ethel Kennedy's biographers.

RFK overheard

and sent a note to Newfield
Maybe you can talk about something else
or you might cost me the nom
and signed it Timothy Leary

Kennedy had offered to stay out of the race
if Johnson would name a "high-level bipartisan commission
to re-evaluate"
   what the U.S. was doing in 'Nam

  Kennedy had suggested members of the commission
  (with RFK a member)

During the Hickory Hill dinner
Kennedy was called from the table
It was Secretary of Defense Clark Clifford
with the answer from Johnson
No commission
   & Kennedy had to enter
      the race to be President.

*Planned in creation/Arouse the Nation*

## After a Reading a Bunch of Us Visit the O

Almost exactly at midnight
we pulled into the
         Beechwood Cemetery
in Gloucester

drove along the rightmost drive
                  to the back
& parked w/ our lights on

to visit the dark slate grave
of Charles and Betty Olson

with its wingéd skull
         engraved
            in the dark.

I kissed the curved top edge
just above the skull

      & said hello again
      to my mentor

Miriam saw a bat lift away
from a nearby grave
          in the headlights

in  this
      "park of eternal events"

## News that Stays News

polis is
eyes

—Charles Olson
letter 6
*Maximus*, I

# Ginsberg

## Ginsberg Reading at the Living Theater Early '59

I liked it that he sort of bubbled out of the '50s
Complete and Bardic
Full Voiced and Howling
I didn't have to know
        really whence he came

but only that he was There
Fully there
Completely there
with a voice I trusted

to lead me to the Best Minds

# Live Free or Die

At Tim Leary's place on November 26, '60
he took some psilocybin
and believed he could cure
Leary's bad hearing
and fix his weak eyes

      Mr. Leary was hesitant
      to allow the naked Irwin Allen Ginsberg
      to roam the streets of Cambridge that night
      in order to preach the Power of Love

      And then came 1961
      the year of the Kennedys
      and Allen donated the handwritten draft of
      "Kaddish" to the Living Theater
            for a benefit

Allen took very seriously
his psychedelic experience with Leary

to the point he felt he had to proselytize
            'cybin's use
    on behalf of a New Consciousness
    and a New Aeon of Thrill-Share & Peace

Among the first of those he turned on to psilocybin
were Thelonius Monk, Dizzy Gillespie, Willem de Kooning,
Franz Kline, & Robert Lowell.

"The Revolution has begun," he wrote to
Neal Cassady as a New Year's salute

## Ginsberg in India

At the end of '62
Peter and Allen split by boat
Calcutta to Benares

There were many more adventures, such as visiting the Taj Mahal,
but it is the tale of how Allen Ginsberg aided
someone left for dead in the streets
            that to me throws forth a giant torch
                        on his humanity

It was early 1963
Kennedy was still alive
The missile crisis had ebbed
and the Cold War seemed likely to decline
            with a touch of grace from peace-minds

One day on a street where humans were left to die
Ginzap came across a guy in the fetal position
wasting away, flies eating the red meat of his wounds—
            a soon and certain visitor to the worms.

There was a red teacup nearby

A.G. washed the cup and offered the gentleman some water
Then he brought him some curried potatoes
            he was too weak at first to eat

Allen then went to the Ganges to wash his clothes
and when he returned the
            dying naked man still lay in the same spot
                        in the light of the sun
He asked a young man what the naked man wanted
and the young man replied that he wanted to be
            carried to
                        the water

— 47 —

Allen and Peter toted him to the river
    and washed him

In the coming weeks they tended to his care
Brought him a mattress
    hired a guy to wash and feed him

Allen finally learned he'd been tortured and had his tongue cut
out by Muslims
    and had a brother on the other side of India

Allen contacted the brother, and the brother came to Benares
Allen then demanded that a local hospital admit the man

and by the time the brother arrived
the wounded man
    was able to leave Benares with his brother by train—

    A classic Allen Ginsberg anecdote

# Justice

Sometimes justice
comes about through fate
Sometimes justice
comes about through
      long-term passion*

Sometimes justice
comes about through Hathor

Sometimes justice
comes about through

Maat

& sometimes justice comes
to grace through

NOTE: "long term passion" As when, 14 years after the fact, Alabama attorney general Bill Baxley tracked down and tried one of the murderers of the children in their choir robes in Birmingham.

the card I saw in Ginsberg's
      kitchen window

## Song for Allen

He was one of my heroes
Where the river of freedom flows
and the blossom of peace grows
Allen Allen Allen has fallen

What a huge and giant brain!
with its hundreds of Blake lines memorized
10,000 vowels of Yeats,
a Catullus or two, 50 pages of Whitman
Milton's "Lycidas," samples of
Sapphic stanzas, vast memories
of his youth & family, gigabytes
            upon infinitudinabytes of naked truth
            above the burning fields of the earth

Ah Allen
your skyrocket mind
up there w/ Sappho & Keats
exploding
        with such a wide, wild corona
out o'er our Little Part of the Milky Way

He was one of my heroes
Where the river of freedom flows
and the blossom of peace grows
Allen  Allen  Allen has fallen

Well, while I'm here I'll
            do the work—
and what's the Work?
        To ease the pain of living.
Everything else, drunken
            dumbshow
            (from "Memory Gardens" Oct. 22–29, 1969)

He was one of my heroes
Where the river of freedom flows
and the blossom of peace grows
Allen  Allen  Allen has fallen

No time to recycle
No time to read the mail
No time to look at the comet
No time to go to the meeting
No time for fabulous images
No time to think
No time to study Egyptian
No time to listen to Berg
No time to go to the rock shop
No time to relive that moment
No time to sort out cosmology
No time to buy a new oar
No time to decipher the glyphs
No time to sort the papers
No time to measure the moonlight
No time to grow the peppers
No time to argue for freedom
No time to dismantle the fear
No time to savor the visions
No time no time no time no time

He was one of my heroes
Where the river of freedom flows
and the blossom of peace grows
Allen  Allen  Allen has fallen

—Woodstock-Venice-Florence-Rome
1997–1998

## For the Memory of Allen Ginsberg


At last
      I weep for Allen
as we play the
"Om Namaha Shivaya" CD
I bought for Miriam at Mirabai

How Allen sang it for us
cling-clanging his finger cymbals
& Peter Orlovsky singing too
when they came back from India
      in 1964

—Christmas afternoon, 2002

# Two Diary Entries for Harry Smith

Sunday 12-1-91

About 8 hours
on "East Village Hippie in King Arthur's Court"

I've been finishing the book of verse,
which Black Sparrow still wants,
                    according to Tom Clark
            (I have till end of December.)

Then Deirdre went back to
                    Albany
            w/ her boyfriend Chris.

And I was dozing—
Allen Ginsberg called
He'd been not at home when Harry Smith
died; Harry had been coughing blood,
and finally a lot came up,
& he died in the hallway at the Chelsea.
They tried to revive him, a crew from St. Vincent's,
but he was gone.
Allen went to hospital morgue
& sat with him. One eye was semi-open
& the other bruised from the fall.
There was a tube still in his mouth,
and a bandage keeping it there,  & blood
on his beard. His head hair was white
& fine, Allen felt it—the head was
still warm.
He meditated, he said, an hour—a Tibetan
tradition apparently.
There'll be a memorial later.
Debbie Freeman had paid off a 3k Chelsea bill
so he'd feel free. Allen thinks he came back
to N.Y. to die. The O.T.O. will hold
a memorial or ritual at Danspace.

2-9-92  Sunday

Up. At 11:30 Mir & I
drove to NYC for memorial
to Harry Smith at St. Mark's Church.
First we met at 3— Tuli, Steve, & I
practiced "Carpe Diem." Tuli, because
of his recent cancer scare, didn't want to
do "Nothing." I ask if it were
because of superstition; he said, "nah."
The Gnostic Mass began at 4. Harry had
been a bishop in the McMurtry branch of the
O.T.O.

It was fairly tame, though a woman
with open top was placed on an altar (by
one of Harry's paintings) & the priest kissed
her bared bosoms, and she licked the
tip of a spear, etc. It was an
interesting ceremony, with the jaded audience
craning its heads to look through the
incense smoke at the partly enclosed
altar. "Are they fucking?" was a question
whispered more than once.

Then at 5, the remembrance of Harry.
P. Adams Sitney particularly to the point, & Jonas Mekas
& Dr. Gross.

We closed the program—
Steve, Tuli, & I (The Fugs)— with
"Carpe Diem" at 7:30 pm.

Then Miriam & I picked up
a Cajun pizza that Phil & Doris
had ordered for us at their Two Boots
Restaurant, & then drove off to
Woodstock to feed the deer.

## An Economy for Those who Dwell in Blake-Light

that's what we need
no war
no hunger
no poverty

lots of freedom & free time
no oppression
& a ten-week vacation for all every year!

so that we can figure out

what is going on

out here in the boondocks

# Poem to a Gnossienne of Erik Satie

*(to be read while listening to Gnossienne # 5)*

This poem is dedicated to Erik Satie for his activism as a young man when he
first moved to the outskirts of Paris, in 1898, and belonged to a a "Radical-
Socialist Committee." This was not long after he composed his great piano
work, the Gnossienne #5.

> The issue of the rose
> so vital to our youth
> shall rise again
>
> It always has
> it always
> will
>
> And it's
> our dance of
> > our lives
> to grow the rose
>
> It always was
> It always will
>
> Ink on paper told me that
> & the rose agrees
>
> It always has
> it always
> will
>
> There comes a time
> when all the
> > petals have to fall
> & yet there's
> > such a place
> where petals
> > never fall

You know, my Erik—
they're the same same place!

Everyone
has a right
to food, a decent place to live, health,

& fun, my Erik,
fun & fun & fun!

The rose haunts
          all of time
it always has
it always will

Meanwhile
all of us fade
to the same
same
anarcho-determinist
post-marxist
place of the sun

in our
furry pajamas

And the rose haunts
all of time

it always has
it always will

# In Praise of William Morris

*Poet, Publisher, Artist, Designer, Furniture Maker, Socialist*

I.

You have to admit he was groovy,
                in the hipster sense (say around 1959)
        this William Morris

He made things, well-limned and beauteous
and sold them in his shop

He had a genius for design and form
a high metabolism and hundreds of projects

He was very very sympathetic to the struggling worker
and was driven to the barricades by the rage-stirring question:
"How could people starve in a culture of plenty?"

On the other ☞ his cash came from
selling luxuries to the well becashed

They still sell his wallpapers in fancy catalogues
Rich people forgive
forays into communism
from the guard towers of the commune of ultrawealth.

In the late 1870s and early '80s
Morris became a Socialist

It was what William Gaunt termed "Pre-Raphaelite Socialism"
        —that "everyone should be an artist"
        as in "art is the expression of pleasure in labour"
        as in why not cut the haikus of Basho
                        on the woodsman's axe

The way Morris saw it the world was riven with Commercial War
State 'gainst State & Seller v. Seller

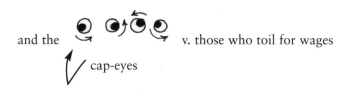

and the                                    v. those who toil for wages

cap-eyes

It was a way of keeping the Machine in Check!
If hand-fashioning could be done as effectively
and pleasantly for the worker
     as by a machine
     then set aside the machine!

2.

King Arthur's Round Table
    so symbolic to the painters and poets
was a paradigm for communism
    it seemed to Wm Morris

who wrote "My business is to stir up revolution"
and so he gifted his skills upon
       the Muse of Pamphleteering

as surely and steadily as, say, George Bernard Shaw
several decades later.

In 1883 Morris signed on with the Democratic Federation
just about the only overt socialist group around

It soon changed its name to the

Social Democratic Federation
to make its politics more translucent


3.

William Morris, to his garlanded praise in the time-track
began to walk the talk

He even sold some rare books to pay for socialist pamphlets

In Socialism he sought the unblemished beauty of religion
                                          and antique form
but of course he ran headlong into the World of Splinters
Careerists and Twisting Factions

and also the brutalized facts of the masses
who even today would have preferred the fumes of NASCAR
to the utter thrill of the Rouen cathedral.

If he had stuck in his lectures to Art
                    it would not have created hostility

but there's nothing quite like raising the banners of the Left
to bring on the snarls of the press, the hostility of acquaintances,
and the dismaying disorder of the Inside

Ahh, factions! How Many Factions can You Fit on the Tip
    of a bookbinder's needle or an etcher's sharp stylus?

Answer: plenty
as many as there are foxéd old pamphlets in the British Museum

4.

Some of the Origins

Thomas Carlyle's 1843 *Past and Present*
on the Chartist movement

in a time of "great industrial distress"

One of the remedies was the concept of escaping
back into the past

to find ideas for reform

John Ruskin writing fiercely of "industrial wrong"
just as writers in other countries
scalded the "political wrong"

William Morris was fueled by the Middle ages
and began to make glass, fabrics, chairs, tables

as if a medieval craftsperson—

𝕽𝕰𝖁𝕺𝕷𝖀𝕿𝕴𝕺𝕹!

as he took the use-rounded antique steps

up toward

S

The path
from the 14th C

that Morris foresaw
as surely as his hand shaped brilliance

The Socialist League

5.

There was a factional dust-devil at the Federation in 1885
as the drive for Socialism gathered people and problems

—something about the secession of a body of Edinburgh
socialists from the Federation

with the result that Wm Morris found himself at the head
of something called the Socialist League

you can look it up in the leaflets
and position papers of the era

6.

Friends were amazed, and some alarmed, that he
was working to destroy the economic system
that saw the ⊚ ⊚⟋⊚⟍⊚          invest in images & art

The art crowd
was like a fluffy salad of talking endives
whose moneyed onions made sure a favored painter thrived.

Down in the garden of art the dancing money lurks
but please don't stand against a war with the Turks

So William Morris left the jive of the endive
the pleasant ride of the scholar-designer
to take the bumpy road from medieval reveler
to analytic Marx and the ancient Leveller

however much for an aesthete and lover of beauty
he perforce had to face the shabbiness and
out-of-luck-and-pluck
        in the big neighborhoods of English cities

7.

### A Stink-Bomb from Right Wingers

In 1885 Morris gave a talk "in a music-room in Holywell"
at Oxford in which he spoke of Socialism

Young right wingers yowled and
beat their feet on the floor at his words
Then they moved toward the stage

Someone had a bottle of a stinky chemical
which they opened and spread in fumes of vom-vom
                                    to kill the meeting

8.

### Bloody Sunday
### November 13, 1887

The weather was bleak and gloomy
of the sort to damp down revolutionary ire

Economic depression had knocked people out of work
The workers were upset

The issue of the Irish and the way the gov't dealt with the Irish
were factors in the disquietude

Thousands were set to converge upon Trafalgar Square
from several directions

William Morris was one of the marchers

The gov't had ordered the police and troops to kill the march
They attacked and sent it scattering
during which one young man, Alfred Linnell,
            was wounded and died a few weeks later

Morris's speech at the young man's funeral

had a theme of bread and roses

25 years before the great strike at the cloth mills of
Lawrence, Mass
            came up with the historic banner
            "We want bread and roses too"

He said, ". . . if society had been differently constituted,
his life might have been a delightful, a beautiful and a happy one.
It is our business to organize . . . to try to make this earth
                        a beautiful and happy place."

That's what we should do
find Alfred's gravesite

and place there loaves and roses day 'pon day
till bread and the flowers of fun
bescent each place beneath the sun


                        9.


Then in 1889 some avowéd anarchists
got control of the Socialist League

and voted Morris out of power

Thereafter, in the words of William Gaunt
it became a "small and bitter sect"

Welcome, o sect, to the tens of thousands of
            leftist hickory cudgels

                gathered in the great cudgel-stands
                of dusty hallways
                by empty meeting rooms

10.

He spent the last seven years of his life
going out in a blaze of publishing

He founded the Kelmscott Press

for which he designed type, selected the best of papers,
and worked with the best artists

His last great work was a famous edition of Chaucer
with Edward Burne-Jones doing the drawings
                              for the woodcuts

Ahh, Sun-Flower, weary of time

It took him five years to publish the Kelmscott Chaucer
—a folio in pigskin with a silver clasp

Yeats termed it the "most beautiful book in the world"

A blaze of publishing so that the socialist publisher
              could die at 62
                    that October of '96

in the monumentality of his time-track.

       Praise William Morris
       but please know this:

       *Great art and socialism*
       *still can kiss*
       *Great art & égalité*
       *bread and bliss*

# By Pont Neuf

*A Meditation on Bad Blood*

Some of the best poets of
    America were sitting at the table
       in the Indian restaurant on E. 6th

Ed Dorn, Alice Notley, Allen Ginsberg, Jerry
Rothenberg, Anselm Hollo, Anne Waldman, Bob
Rosenthal, Bob Holman, and others

It was after one of the symposia celebrating
the 20th anniversary
      of the St. Mark's Poetry Project

I was feeling good
    I'd just ended the evening with
YIDDISH SPEAKING SOCIALISTS OF THE LOWER EAST SIDE
      sliding my hands into the gloves
      of the Pulse Lyre
         to drum sweet tones
           beneath those socialist days
& I had shown everybody the thin plastic handcuffs
I'd kept as a souvenir of the sit-in at the CIA
a few days before.

      Allen was talking about vengeance & bad blood
      He mentioned how someone
      had told him the MOSSAD was behind
      the murders of Indira Gandhi
           and Anwar Sadat—

to block peace

and how he'd thought this was just paranoia till
he brought it up with Burroughs & Ted Morgan
and they didn't think it was that far out of line
(to consider at least)

"It's a terrible problem," he said,
        "Bad Blood," then he chanted:

"The rage-driven, rage-tormented, and rage-hungry troop,
Trooper belaboring trooper, biting at arm or at face,
Plunges toward nothing, arms and fingers spreading wide
For the embrace of nothing; and I, my wits astray
Because of all that senseless tumult, all but cried
For vengeance on the murderers of Jacques Molay."

            Yeats was saying something
            about himself
                    and all of us with quick wits,
            quick words, quick passion, quick ire—
            the rags of a long, slow kerosene fire

        And then a few days later, Miriam & I
        were walking along the towpath
            toward Pont Neuf
to the gray stone bridge and
the plaque marking where Jacques De Molay had
been burned at the stake:

            "A CET ENDROIT
            JACQUES DE MOLAY
            DERNIER GRAND MAITRE
            DE L'ORDRE DU TEMPLE
            A ETE BRULE LE 18 MARS 1314"

*Bad Blood   Bad Blood*
*Born in the Time Flood*


    "It's a terrible problem," he said, with a pause—
    "Bad Blood."

    I remember kneeling
            to join the Order of De Molay

    You weren't given much real history

but a lot of pageant
and the sense that Philip the Fair was
                    batty for the rack.

I once acted the role of De Molay
recreating his final moments—it was
the chance to scream off-stage
while being tortured
            and then to be dragged
through a dark lodge hall
            before a trio of judges
a chance to mix defiance with theism
defy the death robes
            scary moments of myth and martyrdom
heart beating in fear
            though only a play
when the judge shouts, "To the stake with him!"

        Templars were founded in the 12th Century
        military order to protect pilgrims
        to Jerusalem

    In two blood-spackled centuries
    the Templars morphed into warrior-bankers
    with vast treasures in many countries, but
    stood then accused of erotic anti-Christian rituals
            the worship of Baphomet
            and midnight *spuitio supra crucem*
            i.e., ptooeying the cross

        It gave Fair Philip
        a chance to crush them
        bash open the Templars' vaults
        horse-loads of silver
                wending from Spain
                    for the king of France

            It must
            be tied
            to hormone trails,

to urge to raven & venge

it builds, it bobs, it wanes
it fuels the Christian window panes

*Bad Blood   Bad Blood*
*Born in the Time Flood*

I was sitting in the double-benched police van
wriggling my wrists
to pull free of the thin plastic handcuffs

when one of my long time political
enemies,

one that had terrorized me,
smashed the windows of my car, slashed my tires,
was plopped aboard

Jesus!  Can't a guy sit in
at the CIA without

some creepy enemy from the streets
sleazing my wagon?

Ahh, there he is, arrayed in "Hell-is-other-people"
dissplendour
   I feel the same quiet disgust
   as for the CIA guys who stepped over
   us on the tarmac a few minutes ago

*Bad Blood   Bad Blood*
*Born in the Time Flood*

   Old hatreds passed down
   cent' 'pon century

   Your grandfather stabbed mine
   take that!

Sweating the border of a country—
Raging on the edge of a river—
Demanding to know who owns what bream
For how long, and with whom—
To share a doom
            instead of a dream

*Bad Blood   Bad Blood*
*Born in the Time Flood*

Old hate spits late
and the meanness
            in the nursing home
as they ram one another
with canes and wheelchairs
bottles and tubes in arms ajaggling

two old foes—
spitting their hate through sunflower gate

*Bad Blood   Bad Blood*
*Born in the Time Flood*

Slowly the species lifts away
from the crimes of Tantalus,
Thyestes, Zeus, Hera, Medea,
Elektra, Aegisthus, Clytemnestra,
Orestes, Ajax, Achilles, Apollo,
Poseidon, Athena, Agamemnon,
Kleon, Tiberius, the Borgias, Othello,
MacBeth, Pope Clement IV, Mather,
Johnson, Nixon, Reagan, Teller,
et alii toxificandi

Oh Lord, I hope it's soon enough

for at the edge of the sedge-clumped wetland
the squirrels bite off the red maple flowerlets
to drink the sap    while below

the truck of chemicals
dropped there last year from a crack lab
oozeth
down upon the swaying mass
        of salamander eggs
      in a pool among the tussocks
    like thousands of little green grape hearts
in a sac of aspic

That's us

   *Washing our blood*
   *Born in the Time Flood*

## To the Revolutionaries Not Yet Born


I & all my comrades
    will falter, fail, fall
        with the task unfin'd

but I call out to all the Workers of the Rose
to you, o Revs of the Morrow
Take it onward!

Declare it!  Name it!  Work it!

        a Permanent
        cradle-to-grave society of the Sharing Rose

        w/ freedom to speak, dream, act,
                                    & create

a place where there is no poverty
                    no class structure
and everyone has equal access to
                    the best medical care
where there is genuine protection of the environment
an organic food supply
        & lots of personal freedom


That's it, o Revs of the Morrow
Work in extra dimensions
Think 100 years ahead
Enjoy your Revolution
Show enough mercy so
        that Mercy shows the way
& never give up till
            war-hungry capital is gone
            & the Fields of Sharing prevail

## You Have to Be Ready for Ridicule


Leonardo packing up the Mona Lisa in 1516
                    to live near the King of France

*You have to be ready for ridicule*

The plane plops on the beach in 1903 after just a minute

*You have to be ready for ridicule*

You silkscreen Marilyn Monroe all in gold in the fall of '62

*You have to be ready for ridicule*

You get an idea that the continents are all adrift
                    on thick plates of the earth

*You have to be ready for ridicule*

You saw a saucer on the high sands of time

*You have to be ready for ridicule*

You don't think a mall should be built on a meadow

*You have to be ready for ridicule*

You'd like a nationwide, affordable nonprofit
                    health care system

*You have to be ready for ridicule*

# Hymn to the Rebel Café

They were planning a revolution
    to end want and hunger

They were plotting a new form of thinking

They were arguing in blue smoke
    a direction for art

They were friendly and querulous
    chaotic and sensuous

They were ready to fuck
    They were ready to flee
They were ready to fight
    They were ready for jail

They were ready
    to topple the towers

    in the Rebel Café

    Hail to the Rebel Café
    Hail to the Rebel Café

The poet
    came in a skiff
        across the Nile
with satires in his pocket
    on long flakes of stone

The metalsmiths came from their shacks
in the Valley of the Kings

The priestess-singers
    sneaked away
from the Temple of Amon

to play the long necked lute

while the painters passed around
their rebel art
            on rolls of papyrus

They came from all around
to the linen tent
            by the half-finished temple

They came for a whiff
of chaos and mating, lust and leisure
music and art

They came to laugh at the pharaoh
and all of his snitches
They came to the Rebel Café

All hail to the Rebel Café


The Philadelphia taverns
                of 1776
were rebel cafés

Thomas Jefferson and John Adams
            talking about the Declaration of
                Independence in the
                    City Tavern

or Benjamin Franklin
            in his fur cap & spectacles
Thomas Paine
            in a three-cornered blue
lifting pewter tankers in the Indian Queen
the night a pamphlet called *Common Sense*
                            came off the press

They were drawing a nation with ink
                inside the Rebel Café

All hail to the Rebel Café

Twenty-five Yiddish speaking socialists
left the Tomashevski Theater
on a June night
in 1894
and packed
the front of the
Café Royale
on 2nd Avenue

planting
the orchids
of sharing
for 200 years
in the moil of a Rebel Café

All hail to the Rebel Café

Gérard de Nerval
walks with a lobster on a leash
into the Rebel Café

All hail to the Rebel Café

Max Jacob, Pablo Picasso, Guillaume Apollinaire
meeting each night to talk
and to plot
in Austin's Fox Bar, Paris, 1904

All hail to the Rebel Café

—da da da da—
Five poets chant at once
—da da da da—
the world's first simultaneous poem
—da da—
in the Cabaret Voltaire
—da da—

1916
—da da—
Zürich
—da—

All hail to the Rebel Café

Jean-Paul Sartre
        sitting with Simone de Beauvoir
                in the Café Flore
                waiting for Hitler to fall
                in 1944
All hail to the Rebel Café

Janis Joplin
        leans against the bar
            with a guy from Detroit, a
                    guy from Texas,
                    and a guy from
                        Salem, Missouri
            to sing "Amazing Grace"
                in the Rebel Café

All hail to the Rebel Café

Hail to the Stray Dog, to the Caffé Trieste!
Hail to thee, o Total Assault Cantina!
Salutes, o Greater Detroit Zen Zone!
Hail, o Sempiternal Scrounge Lounge of Topeka!
Hail to Dusey's Truckstop!  To the Silent Fiddle Moon Tent,
to Manducca's on Avenue B, to the Golden Bard
Retirement Home's
                Saturday Night All Thrills Café!

All hail to the Rebel Café

    We'll have to keep on
    opening & closing our
    store fronts, our collectives,
    our social action centers

till tulips are in the sky

The cafés come    The cafés wane
but the best and the final rebel café
is inside the human brain

All hail to the Rebel Café
All hail to the Rebel Café
        Rebel Café

# Aeschylus

# Aeschylus Is Waiting

### 1.

The poetry of Aeschylus
is lurking there, outside of cribs,
waiting for you to recognize its genius—
text in hand looking up those obscure Greek words
in your *Liddell & Scott*
chanting it like Yeats in the evening
as he tapped his fingers on the arm of the chair
checking a line by saying it—

looking for the key to complicated meters
of Cretics, Ionics, & wild patterns of
short syllables followed by a long

The only word
for it is
  beauty

### 2.

Ahh, Aeschylus!  How baffling is your singing!
your throbbing chants—so murky & brilliant—
cause us to ask what is it
with the gods?  What is going on?
Just as, 2,500 years later
cosmologists seek to tell us
how many dimensions there are
(maybe 11, or 7 across a p-brane)
& will everything slide back
to a dinky little Planck unit where
not even Zeus is allowed?

*Aeschylus! Aeschylus!*
*Chant for us, throb for us*

3.

He believed in the ancient myths
& pondered the deities with a kind of verse-stunned awe

He knew all those antique tales
How the Greeks looted island to island
                        on the way to Troy

And strove with brilliant meters
        to link the red passions of hoplite & king
        to the red rings of gods and bloodline curses
        that seem at first like unearned suffering

How vengeance
        gives birth to vengeance
blood upon blood

so that the ball of ancient curses
        bounces

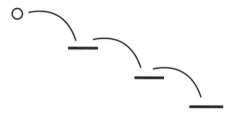

                down the marble staircase
                        of the generations.

Maybe he was trying to explain
the Universal Weirdness in ways
that clarified the Eleusinian Mysteries
and the surge of endless war.

And what about these deities
that liked to date humans, that thirsted for obeisance,
that yearned to sniff the caustic fumes of city-burn,
boat-sink, and the sacrifice of innocent lambs?

4.

He was born at Eleusis in 523
7 years older than Pindar, the Theban Eagle

He took part in the wars against Persia
started placing his poems in the contests
and won his first first in 484

He produced & acted in his own plays
whose expenses were paid by the Athenian state
He may have been stricter than Samuel Beckett
in the planning of his plays
& few poets have been able to
            translate the marvels of his lines

In tragedy he introduced the second actor
and thus made true dialogue come to life on the stage
His productions utilized elaborate costumes
which in turn inspired
            the use of costumes in the Eleusinian Mysteries

The plays we have are from the final 16 years of his life
In 458 he won the glory with the *Oresteia*
            & two years later he passed away at Gela in Sicily

By his death, Athens had bested the Persians
and was strutting the seas
            with her pushy boats

Not far ahead she would screw up badly
in a long and creepy war against Sparta

5.

**Aeschylus Gets into Trouble**

Aristotle (in the *Nicomachean Ethics,* iii, 1, 17)
mentions that playgoers in Athens
attacked the poet maybe during or right after
a performance of one of his plays

accusing him of revealing one or more of the secrets
of the Eleusinian Mysteries

(Through his wealthy family back in Eleusis
he may have been more connected
with the mechanics of the Mysteries
                    than we can know)

Aeschylus took refuge at the altar of Dionysus

                    (the Greeks were loath
                    to kill
                            in sacred places)

and members of the Areopagus of Athens
(the body which tried felony cases)

intervened for him, begging the crowd
                    not to slaughter the bard
                    promising he'd be brought to court.

*(The Scholium of Eustratios,* p. 40,
indicates the plays in question
were *Archers, Priestesses, Iphigeneia,* &
*Sisyphos.)*

## 6.

"Will he have 3-D in time?"
William Burroughs once asked on a T-shirt

Are the gods truly dead? O Aeschylus
O William! as I ponder how darkly difficult
the choruses of Aeschylus are
tied or not tied to Zeus' star
with or without the deeds of the Medes
We can never say good-bye
to Aeschylus & his poesy sublime
hinting at the Mysteries to the grrrs of the crowd
in the 3-D of time

## The Aeschylean Upsettedness of the People

They say the English masses were so angry
at the Germans after World War I
  they demanded harsh reparations

of the sort that fueled the rise of the right
and the Beerhall Putsch

Is that so?

The people can rise to a boil
    that's for sure

Recall the lines of Aeschylus in *Agamemnon*
when a herald has announced the fall of Troy

and the nervous chorus of elders tosses forth
some unsettling matters with Klytemnestra

such as

"Powerful is the voice of the people stirred with anger
It has the strength of a whole nation bound as one"

Aeschylus knew how the people can boil
but can they boil toward aught but war?

I don't know   Clio doesn't know   Helen is unaware
Gandhi wasn't sure   the Kennedys thought it could

and it's our only chance

## Robert Kennedy Recites from *Agamemnon*

His plane was in the air
with tentative word
It landed in Indianapolis
where he found out for certain

He was making a campaign stop
The Indiana primary was a few weeks ahead

He drove to the rally
about a 1000 supporters
who hadn't yet heard the news

RFK then delivered a spontaneous encomium
in praise of Martin Luther King
to a stunned audience

which included these lines:

"My favorite poet was Aeschylus.
He once wrote
'In our sleep
pain
which cannot forget
falls
drop by drop upon the heart
until
in our own despair
against our will

comes wisdom
through the awful grace of God'"

He'd first read those words
a few months after Dallas
when Jacqueline Kennedy had shown him Edith Hamilton's
*The Greek Way*
He read it carefully, also Hamilton's *Three Greek Plays.*

Did King's death alert Robert Kennedy to the danger
out there in the gun-batty darkness?
or did it make him more quietly fatalistic
in the walled words of Greece


I decided to take a look at the ancient text
which comes in the midst of a 223-line chant
near the beginning of the play

A chorus of elderly men by the palace
fills in the audience
          on the Trojan wars
               & the karmic knots & curse-based calamities
                    that were soon to befall Agamemnon
                    and the Trojan princess Cassandra
                         whose boat was about to dock
at the end of the long bay near Argos on the Peloponnesus.

The chorus approaches Klytemnestra
to learn about the news,
          given by a signal-fire
               that Troy had fallen.

In the original Greek
the lines that Kennedy spoke
are mainly delivered in cretics — ‿ —
               and iambics ‿ — ‿ —
plus one example of the meter known as
the dochmiac, used for times of high emotion
‿ — — ‿ —  & a spondee! — —

$$\overline{\phantom{-}} \cup \overline{\phantom{-}} \mid \cup \overline{\phantom{-}} \cup \overline{\phantom{-}}$$

τὸν φρονεῖν βροτοὺς ὁδώ–

$$\overline{\phantom{-}} \cup \overline{\phantom{-}} \mid \cup \overline{\phantom{-}} \cup \overline{\phantom{-}}$$

σαντα τὸν πάθει μάθος

$$\overline{\phantom{-}} \cup \overline{\phantom{-}} \mid \cup \overline{\phantom{-}} \cup \overline{\phantom{-}}$$

θέντα κυρίως ἔχειν

$$\cup \overline{\phantom{-}} \overline{\phantom{-}} \quad \cup \overline{\phantom{-}} \mid \cup \overline{\phantom{-}} \cup \overline{\phantom{-}}$$

στάζει δ᾽ ἐν θ᾽ ὕπνῳ πρὸ καρδίας

$$\overline{\phantom{-}} \cup \overline{\phantom{-}} \mid \overline{\phantom{-}} \cup \overline{\phantom{-}} \mid \overline{\phantom{-}} \cup \overline{\phantom{-}}$$

μνησιπήμων πόνος; καὶ παρ᾽ ἄ–

$$\overline{\phantom{-}} \cup \overline{\phantom{-}} \mid \cup \overline{\phantom{-}} \cup \overline{\phantom{-}}$$

κοντας ἦλθε σωφρονεῖν;

$$\overline{\phantom{-}} \cup \overline{\phantom{-}} \mid \cup \overline{\phantom{-}} \cup \overline{\phantom{-}} \underline{\cup}$$

δαιμόνων δέ που χάρις βί–

$$\overline{\phantom{-}} \overline{\phantom{-}} \mid \overline{\phantom{-}} \cup \overline{\phantom{-}} \mid \cup \overline{\phantom{-}} \cup \overline{\phantom{-}}$$

αιος σέλμα σεμνὸν ἡμένων

—*Agamemnon*, lines 176–183

What ARE these vowels and consonants?
The Greek is very very difficult

Ahh, Robert Kennedy!
    what a thorny cluster of lines
    the bard has made
    his Argive elders chant!

In his translation of *Agamemnon*
Robert Lowell
elides together some 23 lines
(including those the grief-numbed Kennedy spoke)
into three:

    Glory to Zeus, whatever he is:
    he cut off the testicles of his own father,
    and taught us dominion comes from pain!

And Ted Hughes in his translation
does lines 176–183 as follows:
        (as best I can determine)

    The truth
    Has to be melted out of our stubborn lives
    By suffering.
    Nothing speaks the truth,
    Nothing tells us how things really are,
    Nothing forces us to know
    What we do not want to know
    Except pain.
    And this is how the gods declare their love.
    Truth comes with pain.

Not nearly as true to gnarly Aeschylus
as RFK.


The poet who visits
        the orginal chorus
runs into the wall-like obstinance of genius

You have to pound it
verb by verb, and image by image
into your pain-hardened brainland

But even after a long and pounding study
how can a bard translate these lines
with their cretics, iambs, and dochmiacs
in the starkness of current strife & war?

        (& did the medieval copyists
        get all the verbs and endings exact?)

I decided to translate a larger section of the chorus
beginning a few lines before the
        ones Kennedy chanted that stunned afternoon

to try to understand:


Oh Zeus! whoever he is!
(if this to him is a pleasing
name to be called)

This is how I name him
and I am unable to come up with any other
when I ponder it fully
except Zeus, and so it's meet to
hurl this follyful idea
        out of my mind.

Whoever once was great
teeming with war-hunger
shall not be said to have ever been alive,
while he that later grew
as a conqueror of land
        has come and gone

But someone who sound-mindedly shouts
victory chants to Zeus,
he shall build a wisdom of the All—

for Zeus, by leading mortals to
think things over
sets them on a useful road:

knowledge comes from suffering
in magisterial mightiness!

It drip drip drips    in sleep
in front of the heart

—the relentless memory-pain—
so that even against our will
a wisdom of soul comes upon us!

thanks to the violent grace

of our divinities
in their sacred throne-place of rule
(their σέλμα σεμνὸν)

—lines 160–183


Be careful, o Robert Kennedy
Please do not venture forth
with the scars of Aeschylus
making you heedless of the fatal anger

# Poetics

## The Egyptian "Sesh"

The Egyptian word "sesh"
the noun for writing or book
and the verb, to write or to paint

shows some of an ancient scribe's apparatus:

a roll of papyrus
a palette with two cakes of ink or paint

a water jar,

and a narrow pen-case
connected by a string
            with which the writer
could carry them in hand or over the shoulder
that they not disperse

You need to create your own "sesh"
or writer's tools
and keep them at hand around the clock—
for there are no weekends for poets.

There's an in-the-field sesh
and an at-home sesh

but you should always have paper and pen
or pencil, knife, scissors, glue, tape,
magnifier, binoculars,

and maybe sometimes a pH tester,
sample bag, camera, tape recorder,
laptop, palmcorder, geiger counter,
nature guide, water colors,

the point is, figure out your own,
and always have it at hand.

# Multi-Decade Research Systems

A multi-decade research project
with its attendant data systems
can be a wondrous structure
to strengthen your art

It can kiss your work
Help you dare
        be part of the history
                of your time & place

After all, a career lasts 60 or 70 years
and a multi-decade research system
of proper magnitude and design
can assist
        in bundles
             of projects
                    year after year

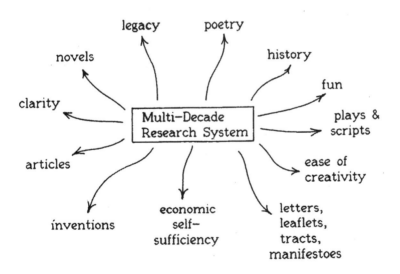

## Paths Through the Data-Clusters
## in the Search for Brilliant Verse

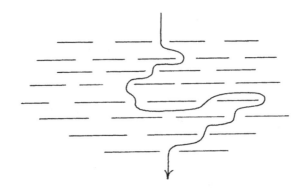

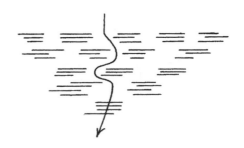

# Sequencing: Key to the Data-Cluster

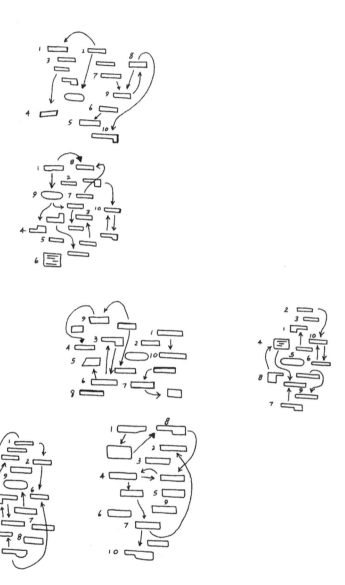

## Investigative Advice from Larry Larsen

"Speak to the
coroner's staff"

—that is, get information also
from the periphery

"No is never really no"

—a no to an investigator
is really a "conditioned yes"

and that "a no with elaborations
always tells you something"

"Make sure your crime scene details
—your details of how
the police work was conducted—
are accurate"

And this:

"The older a
case the
more likely you are
to get information"

# Topos, Typos, Tropos, Tromos

*—for the memory of John Clarke*

*"The basic trio wld seem to be: topos/typos/tropos, 3 in 1,"*
*said Charles Olson*

topos for place
typos for the stamp or mark
tropos the bent, the turning

To which I would add tromos
the green-as-grass trembling

that Sappho felt
at the sight of
Brochea

# The Muses

"Pound's Melopoeia, etc.—Amazing to have
forgotten Noopoeia—revelation . . ."
—from *An Adequate Vision:
A George Oppen Daybook*

1.

Pound famously divided poetry into
Phanopoeia, Melopoeia, and Logopoeia.
to which I have added Tromopoeia
                    & Oppen Noopoeia

How about Mythopoeia?

2.

The Ancient Muses were tied to ancient skills:

    Euterpe   lyric poetry  flute playing
    Calliope   epic poetry   wax tablet and pencil
    Thalia     comedy   comic mask
    Melpomene   tragedy   tragic mask
    Urania     astronomy
    Clio     history   a scroll
    Polyhymnia   sacred singing
    Erato   eros    romance, and easily portable lyre
    Terpsichore   choral singing and dancing    the lyre

so that Sappho's limber-limbic Muses
                 were tied to her techniques:

The pan pipes   the seven-string lyre   the arsis & thesis
The hymn on a hill
              from a circle of singers

but ours is the era of captured sunlight & oxide-dappled tape

for which, as I discovered writing "Sappho on East 7th" in 1982
there is a new Muse, Retentia, Muse of the Retained Image

who captures the beauteous flow
of images in the River!

She rushes to the aid of groaning Clio
when scrolls lie thickened and black

Retentia helps you to sort, to soothe, to winnow
as well as to keep, to save, to shape

The Image is safe with Retentia for a million years
till the pulsing fires which torch all lyres

3.

Gather in the minds of bards, O Muses
as many as there are!

Hail to Electric Clio—the Muse of the Chrono-Flow!
Sequentia—the Muse of the Array and the Sequence
Aphorisma—the Muse of the Supercharged Line!
Condensare—the Muse of Pithiness & Condensation!
Neg-Cap—the Muse of Lingering Uncertainty through Many Nos
before encountering a Yes!
Rhea—the Muse of Getting it Done!
Chronohelia—the Muse of Shining Light on the Time-Track
and the Ungnarling and Sleuthing Out of Secrets
in the Dusts of the Undiscovered!
And then the poesy of Sudden Clarification: Sudclar
Secret Mind: Cryptonoeia
Dictation from the Sky (The Rilke Muse): Uranolalia

4.

"The Muses
appear to be
empty
(deserted?)
    cisterns
in a row"
   —Robert Duncan
    Bard College Reading
    10-29-82

Deep ceramic jars in the valley of eternity

How deep?

A million light years

5.

The Muse of Rhyme—
Maybe she's a librarian too long in the stacks
with a list of rhymes and semi-rhymes
she shows you while you're sweating
You could say her eyes are balefully harsh
but she wants your kiss
Then when your pages are done
she crumples up her lists of rhymes and patterns
& ambles to pull shut the stack-light

6.

So, please do not scorn the Muses
as if they were mere pictographs on potsherds

    Sequentia
   Muse of the Data Cluster

    Retentia
   Muse of the Retained Image

Condensare
Muse of Distillations & Essences

Neg-Cap
The Muse of Patterns of Yes/No

& Ancient Clio
Muse of the Elegant Chrono-Track!!!

## Hymn to Glyphs

Shapes have power
      to shake the spirit
and the bard can draw those forms
for use in the flow of vowels and consonants

since the Visual is rising in the Mix
& glyphs can tremble the brain
or even help bring alive the structures of gnosis!

The promise of a new living hieroglyphic
is of a similar order
as when the ghost of William Blake's brother
gave him the idea for
      reverse copper etching
        & the *Songs of Innocence*

Faces and visual determinatives
as in the ancient Egyptian
can come to verse.

A glyph instead of a name
in a story poem, for instance,
or totems for towns
      in lieu of the letters.

All my bardic life I've drawn them!
It began in 1961 when I was in jail studying Egyptian
after trying to board a Polaris submarine
      in a peace demonstration
when I made flash cards
    in my cell
      to learn the ancient words

such as      and

and then for the next forty-five years
I drew glyphs all the time
wherever I was: on planes, in discussions,
at political meetings, anywhere and everywhere
in quick, instant flows of my many pens!

O glyphs
please enter my visual pathways
and form yourself into my spirit

O glyphs
fire my neurons with beauty-path

O glyph of the ancients
who sought to feel a numinal shape
please enter my skin
     my heart    the soft strip
                    where visual artifacts form
O glyphs   

commingle with my pen
          and come up with the shapes
         that empowered the dawn

I believe  I believe
where the glyph points  

I sail my book-boat

## Emotive Typography

The Eye 𓁹 is sailing ever upward! ⟶

It's in the ascendancy
in such a data-retentive era.

The Eye & its Brain can recognize
around 1,488 hues and shades
& so now may be the time
to use emotive color in verse

As Matisse said over fifty years ago:
"Colors win you more and more.
A certain blue enters your soul. A certain red
has an effect on your blood pressure.
A certain color tones you up. It's the
concentration of timbres. A new era is opening."

So we may see a hieroglyphization of poetry
The Egyptians believed their glyphs were actually alive.
Now life can be resembled, when glyphs can pulse,
can seem to move, twirl, blink elide, change color,
                            erase, erode, and mutate.

Faces, flowers, and parts of the anatomy
in full and subtle hue
could be among a bard's living fonts

Or we may see "mood typesetting"
as when some kinds of music
set moods in movies

Serifs are mental hooks
They help hook words into memory
so why not subtly colored & shaped serifs
                    to bring out moods & emotions?

Each bard with her own brand of serifs & colors
as a painter who has a special brush stroke
                          color palette or "look"
in the shaping of mood, emotion, pace, & nuance

    Call it Emotive Typography
    It's a new way to write
    though it still has to be there
    in pure black and white!

# The Long Voyage Home

# A Sequence of Glyphs

I.

R. Crumb
on his lonely
Rapidograph journey

2.

The Glyph of Peace, Justice, & Social Democracy.

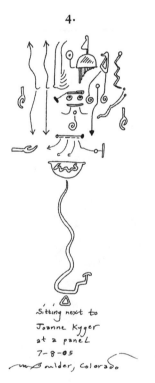

Sitting next to
Joanne Kyger
at a panel
7-8-05
Boulder, Colorado

5.

Out of the
Penetralium of Justice
comes Help-Hand

6.

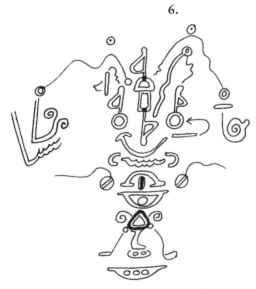

The Celestial Golf Game
Continues

whether or not
there is an equal number of
bosons & fermions
in the Universe

Hands Holding
Peace—
a glyph for
Elin Paulson

8.

It wasn't just you, o Cowper
singled out for Sky Pummel

The cricket
trapped
in the sink
is singing

" I am singled too "

Hekh
The Eternity
of the Sky

Djet
The Eternity
of the Earth

Long Live the Universal
Republic !!

10.

keep clean your shrines
& your Inner Lake

11.

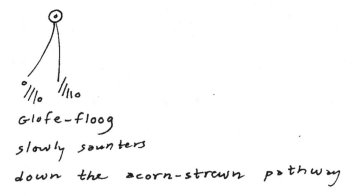

Glofe-floog
slowly saunters
down the acorn-strewn pathway

## 12.
## The Focusing of the Feather

Yet when I read
Blake's Jerusalem

it comes into focus

## 13.

## The U.S.-Supported Ultrarightwing Countries of Condor

A good portion of South America

14.

The Ghost of a May Fly
seeks the remains of its legs & wings
from 1914

15.

You say it was
"too much work"

But the
Hopi Rain Hat
disagrees

what does
it mean --
it means
grace is possible

## 17

The Peace Eye Bookstore
Birth place of the Fugs

Long gone are the Eyes
that guarded the store

yet the Eye of Horus
stands forever healed

## For the Scholar-Activists

Some are happy in a quiet room
weaving maps with Clio's loom
Some are satisfied with graph and list
but not the Scholar-Activist

Months bent down on a screen or page
like a monk in a stoic cell a-rage
till you burst out laughing to the Polis tent
planting the Banners of Betterment

Keep knowledge New o Activists
Know the Fresh Facts First o Scholars
Before the story is flung to freeze, o Scholar-Activists

Don't hesitate to Stare at Forever
for such a viewing shall deliver you a Boat with a Truth-Tinged Sail!

And do not be afraid to forge a wand of adamant
to lead an orchestra of facts on the Polis Green!

Get ready for Derision! But ready too for the Blinding Light
that Plato spoke about in Book 9, o Scholar-Activists!

Cast off thy cloaks of dark, data-soaked Remorse, o Scholar-Scribes!
Rise o Activists shaking your scrolls that burn without harming!
Roll forth, o Scholars! some of you
            may wind up in prison
            for confronting the military-industrial-surrealists

        or those who would murder water and air

Do not despair! for Victory often arrives with Invisible Letters!

        If some of you fall in your blazes of leaflets
        Like the Gracchi or the miners of Colorado!
        Let your names be recorded

in the legends told to children
for 500 years!

I am beating on a bottle of Mental Burgundy light years across!
to shout your emergence, o Scholar-Activists!

Go! S-As, Go! Go! "Build thou Now the Betterment!"
That's what the crack in the bell is singing!
Move your galacto-gluts through the channels of time, o Scholar-Activists
till you lay down your gigabyte burdens
to kiss the fragments of Gaia and the ground-up volumes of star!

## Ode to Rachel Carson


*The Sea Around Us* was published in '51
& won the National Book Award and the Burroughs Medal
It sold over 250,000 copies that year
& made her a national treasure

She'd been one of the first women to hold an upper position
with the u.s. Fish and Wildlife Service.

In early June of 1960 she served on the
Natural Resources Committee
of the Democratic Advisory Council

and listed for the committee the issues she thought most vital:
pollution control, radioactive contamination of the sea, chemicals
poisoning the air/water/land,
preservation of wild space
and the Wilderness Bill:
let's get it passed.

That was the year
she suffered the irony of researching a book
tracking the relationship
of pesticides & disease
while she herself fell prey

She'd been surging ahead in her book
encouraged by her editor at the *New Yorker*
William Shawn

when in January of '60
her doctors found a duodenal ulcer
& then, the same month,
viral pneumonia
& a sinus infection

In March she discovered
several cysts in her left breast
& she was to go to surgery in DC

On April 4 they operated
    & then doctors recommended a mastectomy

She asked her Doctor about
the cysts
she was told she "had a condition
            bordering on malignancy."

There had been a metastasis
            but she was not told

There was no radiation
    & lymph nodes on the left side were removed.


Determined to finish her book she began
dictating changes in the manuscript
which an assistant
        would type

That November, her literary agent Marie Rodell liked the chapter on birds
& suggested that the whole book might be
            titled *Silent Spring*

            Then, ghastly,
            in late Nov 1960
                she discovered a hard swelling
                on the 3rd or 4th rib
                    by the mastectomy

        a dense mass 'tween rib & skin

    so that within days there were
        2 radiation treatments
            then in late January '61
            she was sterilized & received

ten more treatments
                    through February

She began
working again
    on *Silent Spring*
        by the summer of '61
                    in Maine


—Maine always energized her.

Back in Silver Springs, MD
in the late fall
        she shoved herself harshly
                    to finish the greatness

        polishing the "fable for tomorrow"
                    which begins the book.

    By year's end she was sick again
    almost blind with iritis
                & in pain

    but struck onward
    so that by the end of January '62
    she sent
    15 of the 17 chapters
    to her publisher Houghton Mifflin
    & the same to the *New Yorker*

    Shawn loved it
        & wanted to publish it
                    in the spring o' '62


    While polishing & revising
                    revising & polishing
    in March
    she discovered
    a few hard, hurtful lumps

in the lymph glands on her right side

A biopsy gave the grim news
            of another cancer, to the right

So that mid-March
Rachel Carson began
            more radiation

She worked on *Silent Spring*
in bed in the mornings
& then to the hospital for radiation
                        in the afternoons

She was nauseous by midday

And then, April 20, 1962
*Silent Spring*
    in the agony of its creator
                was done!

*It was a moment for America*

She ordered a wig
so that she could start interviews, speeches,
                    and appearances
                    to stand by the science
                                of her book

Then, an enlarged
& painful node in her armpit
& soreness
    in her neck & spine

The installments of *Silent Spring*
began in the *New Yorker* on June 16
            creating a culture-shaking stir

The publication occurred
in the public anger over

thalidomide

The chem-companies
        fought back
but JFK's Secretary of the Interior
Stewart Udall
        backed Carson's book

& advocated
        for pesticide regulation
                in the New Frontier
                        that summer

*Silent Spring* was a Book-of-the-Month Club selection
& went on sale in stores September 27, 1962

        There was a huge huge flood of press interest & interviews
        & considerable hostility from conservatives
                                and chem-sleaze.

A pesticide industry ooze-group
spent over $250,000
        to attack Carson & her work

She was picked on as just an alarm-ringing woman
sort of a Cassandra of chemistry

The press was very attentive to her marital status—
that is, single
        with the Cold War implication:
        Communist, &, like, Sapphic

        and the fact that she had "only" a Master's Degree

Then, December '62
terrible pain
        in her back
with *Silent Spring* #1 on the *New York Times* best seller list
most of the fall
        and during Christmas

she went through radiation treatments
                              on her back

During the increasing hubbub from chem-sleaze
Carson was always ill
yet worked hard
        answering critics
            doing outstanding stints on television
            making excellent speeches
                    & shaping the PR battle

Then new lymph tumors
            above the collar bone
& another in her neck
            in February o' '63
        after which another series of heavy radiation

She began suffering from angina
            in the spring of '63

The federal government issued a report on May 15, 1963 called
"The Use of Pesticides"
        by the President's Science Advisory Committee


        By September
        of '63
        it was too painful to walk
        from "the pain in the bones of
        her pelvic girdle"

    yet she kept up her fierce Icy Fight
    with the Scythe Man

    till by March 13, '64
        the disease entered her liver

    & then on April 14, 1964
    Rachel Carson passed away
                of a heart attack

2/3 of her estate she gave to the Nature Conservancy
& to the Sierra Club

& you can pause by her monument
on a street in Booth Harbor, Maine
to know the Hokusai churning
of The Sea Around Us

# The Right Wing Crushes the
# Great Henry Wallace

*—Diane di Prima wrote me after she read "The Right Wing Crushes the Great Henry Wallace": "The Henry Wallace poem recalled for me Charles O telling me (we were both tripping) about the finagling to get Truman the Vice Presidency—and how they were sure* FDR *would die I'm sure he told you that story—the facts are a blur now—I was glad you wrote what you did about it—What isn't a blur is Charles' imitation of* FDR *with almost no motor skills left trying to get a cigar to his mouth—What an actor* CO *was!"*

## Wallace as Vice President
### 1940

Vice President John Garner
    had opposed Roosevelt running for a 3rd term
    so the President dumped Mr. Garner
    and pressured the
    Democratic Convention in Chicago that July 19
    to nominate the plant geneticist Henry Wallace
        who used to publish the newspaper, *Wallace's Farmer*

Wallace had been the Secretary of Agriculture since '33
    running the New Deal assistance programs
                    to farmers

The right wing hated him
    and slowly, during the following years
        formed a Get Wallace! fang-pack

## The Question of What Kind of Century?
### 1941

A human being named Henry Luce
owned several powerful magazines
including *Life* where early this year
he published an editorial
    called upon an American Century
based on capitalism as opposed to "utopian dreams of social reform"


a Pax Americana
    of money hunger & a We Know Better empire.

Henry Wallace answered with "The Century of the Common Man"
a New Deal for all the world through democracy


## Hating Henry Wallace
### 1944

The eyes of disapproval
    among conservatives
        began to focus on the
    liberal plant-geneticist vp Henry Wallace
    next in line

and party bosses began to mutter, "Get him out of here."

All that spring and summer
hubrisistic hacks hacked heartily
    to gouge Henry Wallace from the ticket

FDR wanted Wallace to
    work better with the Senate
and the big business Wall Streeters and crypto-conservatives
the President had brought in
    to help run the war
    wanted the New Deal intervention over.

It's a complicated tale.
There were a few powerful New Dealers that wanted
William O. Douglas to step away from the Supreme Court
              and run for VP

But I think it was the National Democratic Chair
from the St. Louis machine
    (close to Senator Truman)
    who did the most to snuff Wallace from the fray

You can look it up
        in the many Henry Wallace time-tracks.


### The Concept of a New Party
Summer

FDR sounded out Mr. Wendell Wilkie
        on forming a new Liberal Party

    so as to escape the right wing sludge in the Democrat Party
    & the howling, hating, hubrising Republicans

Wilkie had been defeated by the conservative wing o' th' Rep's

so that July FDR sent his trusted speech-writer/confidant Sam Rosenman
to talk with Wilkie

the plan was to commingle the liberal parts of the Democrats
with the liberal parts of the Republicans

        Wilkie liked the idea

On July 13 FDR dictated a letter inviting Wilkie
    to the White House or Hyde Park

    but someone snitched the letter to the media
    where it created an ink-squall so that
    the meeting was put off till after the election

(Wilkie, however, died that fall
and so history was denied)


## Roosevelt & Truman
### July 19

Roosevelt came in his private train to Chicago
for the Democratic Convention

Big time pols are a bit like wolves
& I think the Dem-wolves
felt FDR soon would pass
& that the VP would be the president

so it was grrrr
get Wallace
out of here
grrrr


Senator Harry Truman of Missouri looked good to them
though some wanted Supreme Court Justice William O. Douglas
& James Byrnes (later Truman's secretary of state)
truly hungered for it

Wallace had a lead on the first ballot
but Truman swept into place
on the second

setting the stage for the dropping of the a-bomb


## Left! Right! Left! Right!
### Late 1947

Truman was advised to move to the Left
on domestic policy
to stitch up the New Deal coalition

farmers, blacks, Jews, org labor
&urban ethnics

and then to push the Cold War.
So said a long memo from Clark Clifford
advice which the man from Independence followed.

### The Strength of Henry Wallace
### February, 1948

In the Bronx
a special congressional election
won by a candidate from the American Labor Party
who was pledged to Henry Wallace

A Gallup Poll predicted that Wallace'd get
13–18 percent of New York's vote

### The Faked War Scare of Early 1948

What
Eisenhower in
'61 wd name
the Military-Industrial Complex
entered the "picture"

I shall call them in my poem
the Military-Industrial Surrealists
or the mil-ind-surrs

The military-industrial-surrealists
with their hungers for profits & puissance
pushed forward a pre-planned war scare
early that year

part of which was to force the Republicans
to pass the European Recovery Plan
known in history as the Marshall Plan

which arrived for Truman's signature not long
after
    the war scare had been promulgated
    without any evidence of
        actual Russian war intent

(there had been a Communist coup in Czechoslovakia
which had produced vast alarmist headlines)

For more, you could read Frank Kofsky's interesting
*Harry S. Truman and the War Scare of 1948–*
*a Successful Campaign to Deceive the Nation*


March 17, '48
    Truman at a St. Patrick's Day dinner
        arranged by th' ultra-right-wing Cardinal Spellman said
        "I do not want and I will not accept
        the political support of Henry Wallace & his Communists"


July 15
    Harry Truman was feeling feisty
    in Philadelphia
        at the Democratic Convention
    where Senator Alben Barkley of Kentucky
        was chosen his mate

    "Senator Barkley & I will win this election
    and make these Republicans like it."

July 23–25
    The Progressive Party Convention
        also in Philadelphia
        put forth Mr. Henry Wallace
        for President

    Among the points of the platform:
    •an end to the draft
    •destruction of all a-bombs

•better relations with the Soviet Union

"Wallace or War"
was one of his banners

grr      grrr      grr
went the Republicrats

### Fall 1948 Campaign

When Henry Wallace ran for President
           on the Progressive Party ticket
Truman did what good Democrats have often done
coopted the Left/Liberal
by changing his dance steps
      from hokey-pokey right
      to hokey-pokey left.

He de-emphasized the Cold War
attached himself to a strong civil rights plank in the Platform
called again for National Health Coverage
price controls to help consumers
protection for small farmers
      & repeal of the union-hating Taft-Hartley Act.

At the one-room school I attended in Missouri
      there were rock and mudball fights
          among the children of
              Democrats & Republicans

with the Democratic boys chanting
      "Phooey on Dewey!
      Phooey on Dewey!"

Public opinion polls said Dewey was going to win
George Gallup's final poll on October 30
gave it to Dewey 49.5 to 44.5 percent

### The Wallace Campaign

There was massive red-baiting
of the Henry Wallace-Glen Taylor Progressive Party ticket
        by liberal democrats
        especially by a group called the
        Americans for Democratic Action

(Communists were welcomed into the 1948
Henry Wallace coalition—)

& Southerners who hated blacks
        formed the States' Rights Democratic party a.k.a. the Dixiecrats
        and ran Strom Thurmond of South Carolina for pres

        "Keep America Human with Truman"
           was one of Harry's posters


### Democrats Sweep
November 2

Many Americans believed (back then) that the
        popular vote
                appoints the president
but election night '48 almost showed
how the "electors"
        could have given it to Dewey.

All night Truman surged in the popular count
but trailed in the electoral college
till dawn when
        he won the State of Illinois
            & measured his victory.

        Final tally: 303 electoral votes to Truman
           189 to Dewey
           Thurmond 30
            Wallace   zero

Popular count: Truman 24.1 million to Dewey at 21.9 million

Henry Wallace at 1.15 million
Strom Thurmond, States-Rights Democrat 1.169 million
& the Democrats won both houses of Congress!

(Wallace won 509,559 votes in NY
and the state went to Dewey)

**Labor**

In the end America's working people
particularly those in unions
voted for Harry
to stanch the assault on the New Deal
and the crushing of labor

"Labor did it,"
Truman said in Kansas City
the day after the voting.

—adapted from *America, a History in Verse*, Volume 2

# Independence

I woke up feeling
  "O.K."
      for the first time in a while.

Why? Back pain lessened,
a little $ has come in,
trip to Italy w/ Miriam ahead,
Deirdre home, cold gone
2 books coming out

& "health" seeming
      to get "up there"

And America's
      not at overt war anywhere
(as far as we know).
It's the 4th of July
& I'm celebrating American freedom
& toasting
      the growth of Social Democracy

with my mental bumper sticker

> **Nationalize
> Natural Gas**

—July 4, 1999

## Hymn to the Lower East Side

Hail to thee, o Lower East Side in the Time-Mist!
A million salutes to thee
                    o Rebel Zone of the Age!
Come Alive  Come Alive
        in the Olive Trees of Time!

Bring forth your Labor Day Parades
                            of 1886 & 7
Bring forth your
        million lines of poetry on Avenue C

Bring forth your underground films
                            of Avenue B!
Bring forth
    the mass demonstrations
    during the economic collapse of 1896

Come back again
        o Peter Stuyvesant's farm
        on which we stand today

Flash outward
o drilling ground for
        Civil War soldiers
        headed for the
                skull-studded flood plains of Antietam Creek!

Give up, o Time-Mist
        the flashing art stores of 1982!

Shine again
        o Peace Eye Bookstore
                        & the birth of the Fugs there in 1965!

Whitman forth!
        o Second Street pad of Allen Ginsberg

where he wrote the great "Kaddish"
in 1959

Hail to centuries of spirits
who came to these streets

in the search for a friendly mind
bread for hungry children
freedom from iron-spiked boots
or to flee a pogrom by the Dniester River!

Hail to thee, o Lower East Side!
Long many centuries hence
may you dance, you hammer, you sing, you share, you write,
you paint, you agitate
for a better and peaceful destiny
in a Shining City
on the Harbor of Dreams

—for a reading in Tompkins Park
as part of the *Howl* Festival,
August, 20, 2003

## For Ted Berrigan

We were both using the same
mimeo machine
at the Phoenix Bookshop
in 1963
you for C *Magazine*
I for *Fuck You/ A Magazine of the Arts*

It was obvious
we were slaves
to the lyre and the bee

& we wanted a better
performance
out of our soma

We pranced around
our mimeo machines
like Bassarids

the benzene dripping
from our fingers

& the foxskins
      masking our smiles

You were one of the first
guys
(you and Blackburn)

I met
who lived it
around the clock

and now you're gone
gone too early
and it doesn't matter

now how
we twisted our guts
in the face of the
creator.

Later you ran a series of readings
at the Café Le Metro down the
street from the St. Mark's Church
and printed some of your fliers
at the Peace Eye Bookstore

such as the one you wrote for
May 19 1965:

"JEROME ROTHENBERG
Everybody knows Jerry. His latest book,
SIGHTINGS, cracks the windows of the eyes
with its sonic silence. Better harden yr
heart for this reading."

and this: "MINIMUM 25 CENTS."

You worked your body
for almost half a century
as if you were a vaulter
before a leap

We were combative. We fought
about an issue so stupid it's a blush
to recall.

Maybe this is too personal &
packed with the capital I
to publish
for it's you I want to celebrate.

But I feel a grinding
in my soul.

It's an evil

economic system
that does not
take care of poets.

Sometimes the sky
        drips curses
Sometimes the sky
        drips glee

But a country with a
rotten economic drips
bad times
        for bards

You told me George Kimball
asked you once to a Red Sox game
but that you couldn't go
not owning the proper clothes

It is an
utter &
complete disgrace
that there was
no free national
health system
to which you could
have consulted
            readily
                & easily

America, where bad
teeth cost as much
as a Honda

where poverty
the curse of Chatterton
& Edmund Spenser
still eats
the marrow
        of poets.

I recall the weeping
on the outdoor concrete platform
the echoing "gukh"s
like standing in a cistern

and your daughter Kate
     with striking red hair

her beautiful face
     shining with tears
walked up to place
a single white rose
      on the coffin.

## Melville's Father

"Reputation is far more valuable
than fame or riches"
Allan Melvill

He had a seeking to be stainless

"My children," he wrote
"I trust will inherit an honest name
and keep pace with improvements"


O Name!

O Spotless Clairvoyancy!
Thing of Pure Blood!

O Unsullied Formula
in Time's Torrent!

O spotless
unblemished rivet in
the metal of infinity!

O Stainlessness!


2.

*New York in 1818*

The impoverished
after the Napoleonic
wars

packed NYC

The creeks were paved over,
the farmland taken,

and the poor people's grave blocks
known from the Bible
as potter's fields

became parks
the only spots the developers
would leave behind
as open space


3.

Allan and Maria Gansevoort Melvill,
two spotless names, she of the
purse-proud Gansevoorts
and he of the war hero Melvills
married and bore 8 children.

In 1818
when he was 36
Allan Melvill went to France
to organize a wholesale business
in "French goods"

When he returned
Maria became pregnant
with the future author of
"Bartleby the Scrivener,"
who was born on August 1, 1819

4.

Allan Melvill opened his business
    on Pearl Street
        near the South Street seaport
and supervised the
crates at the docks
    of goods from the schooners
        for the rich and proper:
lavender, ribbons, scarves, handkerchiefs,
selvages (ornamental fringe or ribbon sewn on borders
to prevent unravelling), corsets, bonnets, silk gloves,
fine-plaited wheat straw hats,
Spitafield silk and the fancy cloth
        known as white tapaze.

O French goods!
from the home of Revolution
    the rage of thought!
        the hint of skin!

O triumph of style
that temporary array
    in the torrent, that
meringue above the stratum, where
scents and lace and pheromones commingle
just out of reach of the waves
that slam by Plymouth Rock.


5.


*The Crash of '26*


For eight years it was Triumph!
The ledgers tell the tale,
even though being a middleman
is that most vulnerable
    of roles

But around 1826
    came one of those
    "incomprehensible economic collapses"
those periodic poor-kills
    where they break off city tree limbs
    for firewood
so that the '30s of the 19th
were like the '30s of the 20th,

and French goods were just the
sort of thing
    not to be bought
    during poor-kill.


The Melvills were not prepared
to be swept up in such
    a democratic phenomenon
so, in 1828 they moved with their eight children
and two servants
to a spiffy 2-story house at 675 Broadway
    near Bleecker (don't bother
    to try to find it—it's now a block-
    sized modern brick apartment)


6.

*A Slow Slide*

There's nothing like a
slow slide
    into failure

You think
    sometimes
        it's success

but really, it's

like when
a little commuter
                plane
comes down
                in layers
in a bucking wind,

up, down, down, up
                down, buck

so that failure
        feignedly fastens.


                7.


        For the penniless man
        is the worst kind of criminal
        Beyond both pity and pardon
        —Brecht, *The Rise and*
                *Fall of the City of Mahagonny*

Thou lackest money?
You scum
You are really scum
You are homeless?
You want it that way!
You can't pay?
You are the scum of failure
The scum of scum!
Lower your immune system,
                        scum
Work around the clock,
                        scum
Raise your metabolism
        scum
Burn it! Allan
Shake it! Allan
Make death of it! Allan
Fall with it! Allan

*Shame shame*
*shame & blame*
*never the same*
*stain on the name*


8.

They probably kept it hidden
from Herman and the seven, for

children never want to hear
their parents are out of money—

With rich relatives
it never got down to

recycled clothing under the
Christmas tree

but in those days o' eco-Dickens
                    there was no Chapter 11

and you could
go to jail
    if you fled
        your debts

so when in 1830 Allan Melvill went bankrupt
and they fled their two stories
            on Broadway near Bleecker

there was the click
        of phantom handcuffs
                in the mist

9.

They moved back to Albany
where the cold winter wind
from the narrow Hudson
   was a poor-kill

They tried to keep the horror
hidden from haughty relatives, but he had
  sunk so low as to
    clerk in a fur store.

    Ahh the shame of it!
     Face-burning! Exquisite!
      To clerk in a store!

10.

Advice to the middle aged
    with penury's prize

Save your immune system
Stay calm
Stay energized
Stay cunning, focused
Reach out
Don't blame yourself
It's the system's fault
Be prepared to be sneered at
like a hungry rat
   a run-down cat
     or bat scat

and know that it's
  the fault of
  the same
  cruel system
  formed on the
  edge of the

glaciers
in the
    Pleistocene
      & Holocene


11.


He was almost 50
when the lungs under stress
rasp, "can't do it, can't do it"
    so he tapped into his
        life force.


In April o' '31
Allan confessed poverty to his father


In August o' '31
    he went to Boston
        to ask him (inspector
          of the Custom House)
            for moolah


& then in October a loan from
bro'-in-law Peter Gansevoort
(head of the State Bank of Albany)


for 2k to take over
    a bankrupt retail fur and cap store
    plus a manufacturing plant
    at 364 South Market Street
    (now Broadway) in Albany.


There was plenty of fur
and hides from
the hemlock bark tanneries
        in the Catskills


Allan went to New York City
in late November o' '31

and picked up additional credit—

It was going to be success!
Money!  The Return of Stainlessness!

Servants again!  And the children to be
able "to keep pace with improvements."


12.


The steamboat *Constellation*
       left the New York docks
on an icy December day in 1831
         bound for Albany

He had the money
He had the credit
and contentedly watched the
crusts of ice in the Hudson

eager to get home to make
those beaver hats!
Make some money before Christmas!
Money!

till, 60 miles upstream at Poughkeepsie
the steamer couldn't cut
        through the ice.

They pulled to dock
and there were no covered
coaches available
to scoot up to Albany

A Holocene ice storm
       cares not about a name
so he went in a one-horse open wagon

through bouncy ruts of icy snow

trying to stay on the road

Got to get to Albany!
Not a second to tarry!
Come on Immune System!  Come on Metabolism!

He lost his scarf, and
his coat was warm enough
        to wheel and deal in NYC
but not enough for an
                arctic trail.

The driver
        gave him a quilt
but his lower back froze up

He coughed
                His temperature rose
Good!  More energy!

Here mate, have a shot
                        of hooch
homemade

A cold piece of baked rabbit
to eat

while they fixed the wagon's frame.

Temperature zero.
His lungs felt like they were
full of water.

Thirty miles to Rhinebeck,
then in another wagon to
Hudson— twenty miles

Finally, a covered sleigh to Greenbush
at sunset after
        three hypothermic days

the sleigh let him out.

He walked across the Hudson,
narrow at Albany,
the temperature minus 2 Fahrenheit
in a poor-kill wind
      and went right to his store
            just off the river
                 without going home.

13.

*Mercury*

Melvill was going to "reorganize"
            the fur factory—
on South Market Street
so I ponder whether
      he experimented in beaver felt hats.

They rubbed the felting furs with mercury
mixed with acid

then the hairs were cut from the hide
and put into a pile
which was then
vibrated with a 7-foot bow to shake
           and mold it into interwoven felt—

The trembling bow
would spew mists of quicksilver
         into the hard-breathing
            lungs of the felter

Mercury is extremely nephrotoxic,
causes cellular damage,
it may lead to circulatory collapse
& oliguria, or lack of urine

And those poisoned
    by the feltmakers disease
        could have used dialysis machines
                to cleanse their kidneys.


Mercury inactivates
    a wide variety of enzymes
and aerosolic exposure to it
produces chills, fever, coughs, chest pains,
hemoptysis (blood-spit), insomnia, nervousness,
impaired judgement, propensity to freak out,
fatigue, loss of sex drive, depression, abdominal
cramps, et al.

        It may
        have pushed
        him o'er th'
        Immune
        System
        Edge

For Allan Melvill
evinced some of the symptoms
of mercury poisoning

may literally have gone
        Mad as a Hatter
            striding around his factory

in the neurotoxic wafts
        which are absorbed by the alveoli
and spread to the brain.

In any case
for a month he slaved
consumed with mania and overwork,
his metabolism
        in toxic overdrive
till January 7, 1932

he went bonkers,
        took to bed,
            for twenty-one days
with pneumonia, then delirium, then thanatos.

Herman was thirteen.


14.


*Buy Cheap Sell Dear*

No one
        no group
lives long enough
to structure
        a system
to ease the pain
            of living.


And you can say, well, Sanders,
your analysis
strays from the nature
of the species

and tragedy requires
            the order that is

no rest for the best

but the cruelty of the system
& maybe a little mercury poisoning
killed Herman Melvill's father
                    early.

## The Question of Fame

—The great bard Goethe was 75
when he wrote a friend
he'd never had even a month of
                "genuine well being"

Johann Wolfgang Von Goethe
said he never had any peace
Well, what would it take to make a poet happy?
Is anything ever enough?
It's the Question of Fame
The Question of Fame

An hour and a half
you utter your
        elegant verse

in the packed soccer stadium
                in Santiago
Your poems
are projected
        on dirigibles
                overhead

You're hooked up by satellite
to 300 stadiums
all over the world
and all of them are packed

        —It's the Question of Fame—

Finally you finish
and 30,000,000 people are on their feet
screaming & jogging in place

They clap for hours
till their palms are
        covered with blood

& blisters
pop painfully
        in their shoes

and soon they
        begin to
                thud to the bleachers
like clapping colossi

They lie there hoarsely writhing
the hemic mists still spuming
        from along the edges
                of whacking fingers

their eyes glazed over
like 30,000,000 raccoons
                in a sudden flashlight

This happens every Sunday afternoon
and it's still not enough

## When a Bard Tarries Too Long
## Setting Up His Spring Tour


Quincy Troupe &
Annie Waldman
have sucked up all
the $ at EMU*

    fa  la  fa  la!

I tarried so lately
the shovier bards
took all the cash

    fa  la  fa  la!

Clayton called and
        broke the news
that Quincy and Anne
had each got their 800
plus airfare
the latter which
        seized all the scratch

    fa  la  fa  la!

I should have
    jumped sooner with
        e-mail or fax

& now
    I'll not get to go
        to Ypsilanti
           in the spring 'o '94

    fa  la  fa  la!


*Eastern Michigan U.

## Adventures in the Jack Trade


I told McClure
that Johnny Depp
had paid 15 grand
to Kerouac's estate
for one of
        Jack's jackets

He & Manzarek were
            just about to go on
at Town Hall

&
Ferlinghetti
        was toning
            his final poem

McClure flipped me
the hard Sophoclean eye & said
"I have five or six of those."

"So do I," I replied,
my mind shifting cunningly
from free will
        to Good Will
thinking, of course, that
Depp will need a
2nd coat for when
the 1st is in the cleaners
& another
        for his summer home
            & one for his manse in Nice

# Working with Alf

NOTE: For eight years, I worked as a kind of secretary and research assistant to the historian Alf Evers as he completed his history of Kingston, New York. He was an American genius, and taught me important things about the writing of history. He passed away in late 2004, just a few weeks shy of his 100th birthday, and not long after he had completed his book, *Kingston: City on the Hudson*. Very few humans in their late 90s have ever written any kind of book, much less such a fine and excellent work.

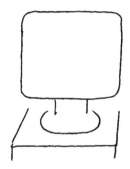

Alf & Tom's cat lies asleep
next to the computer
　　in a box of letters

while I add Alf's corrections
to the years leading up to the
　　　　Revolutionary War


　　　—Sunday afternoon
　　　October 7, 2001
　　　as America begins to bombard
　　　Afghanistan

# Four Butterflies Gone

### William Blake

The last thing William Blake purchased was a pencil
and then that day the Bard continued painting
perhaps to touch up his Dante watercolors
                                        or illustrated Bible

and turned he then to his weeping Catherine
"Stay, Kate!  Keep as you are," he said
"I will draw your portrait, for you have ever been
                                        an angel to me"

He sketched the woman he'd first met 45 years before
& then sang poems and hymns

He told her they would never be apart
            and she would find him always
                        singing by her side

Just before the final flutter, as a friend later wrote
"His eyes Brighten'd and He burst out into
Singing of the things he saw in Heaven."

Then slipped the Bard at 6 p.m.
            to the place where butterflies flap
His friend George Richmond kissed him
            & closed his eyes "to keep the vision in."

### Anton Chekhov

At 2 a.m. the doctor arrived,
Chekhov covered in sweat,
and spotting the doctor
Chekhov sat up,

leaned against his pillows,
and said, "Ich sterbe."

The doctor gave him a
        camphor injection
and was sending for an
                oxygen pillow

but Chekhov said,
"What's the use?
Before it arrives
        I'll be a corpse."

In response Dr. Schwohrer
sent for champagne,
Chekhov held a glass
and said to Olga
"It's been so long since
        I've had champagne,"

and ever slowly drank it down
then lay upon his side

A black-winged moth
had come through the window
and was beating
    its wild wings
            against the lamp.


### After the Funeral

We had stopped at the
        Joyce Kilmer rest stop
                on the New Jersey Turnpike

Miriam wanted to sit near
            the big front windows

so we did

& she spotted a black & white butterfly
that flitted up and down outside
    & then rested on the frame
        right next to us

"I hope it isn't Mother," she said
as we looked at its wing patterns.

She said it appeared
    to be wanting in.

She mentioned Chekhov's butterfly
& the one that appeared when Gerald Durrell
        passed away

"She always said she would haunt us."

We smiled and went back out
    to the ribbon
        that led us home.


### Alf Evers

Just after Christmas day, Alf came down with a cold.
I could hear him cough when we talked over the phone.
Many times those seven years
I had shouted through the deafness,
"Alf! Don't dare get sick!"   & shouted it once again.

I went to his house a couple more times to help
with the final additions to the book
and to locate some of the remaining images

Even with his cold and five weeks shy of his 100th
I noticed he had made a slew of changes
        to the last few chapters!

I called on the 29th and spoke with Tom O'Brien
Alf was singing, Tom said, and speaking as if in a dream.

Later that afternoon, Tom prepared one of Alf's favorite meals,
a bowl of hot oatmeal, which Alf ate almost entirely.

He was quite jovial with Tom, singing and softly talking
                              in a happy voice
Then he went to sleep on his side. It was his favorite position,
the one with the least amount of pain

Not long thereafter a man of glory passed from human life,
not unlike the great bard Blake
who also passed while singing and seeing his dreams before him.

## Matisse

He arose at 7
then played
    the violin
a couple of hours

to loosen
    his fingers
        for painting

# Going to Gregory's Funeral

*I set out now in a box upon the sea. —Charles Olson*


What does it mean
to have been Gregory Corso?
Secure yet insecure, ferocious yet friendly
cruel on occasion & always apologetic,
misogynist & yet philogynist

He was banking
on his sequence of vowels
     & consonants
to carry his legacy

a few poems
frail & strong
    in Olson's box
    on Olson's sea

        —January 24, 2001
        6:50 a.m. January,
        on the Trailways bus
        to NYC from Kingston

# Gregory Said

We talked
　　at Town Hall backstage
Corso & I
(Ginsberg & Vosnesensky
　　　　were standing nearby)

Gregory said
one of the hidden tragedies
of the beat era
was how some parents
seized their beat daughters
and sent them
　　to mental hospitals
for shock therapy.

—something like $50 a day
the parents thought
　　it was good to do.

Seized, locked, shocked—
a hidden
　　scandal
　　　　of the time

# The Ocean Étude

*—to the memory of Jim Morrison*

I asked the guard
    where Chopin was

He said the 11th, up the hill
to the chapel, & to the right

We spotted a hand-jotted sign
on the wall
    of the entrance

JIM MORRISON
**6th Division**

Then we found a building with
a directory. and made a list

| | |
|---|---|
| 6ème | Morrison |
| 8ème | Béranger |
| 11ème | Chopin |
| 18ème | Colette |
| 23ème | Ingres |
| 24ème | Corot |
| | Daumier |
| 48ème | Balzac |
| 49ème | Delacroix |
| | Nerval |
| 85ème | Proust |
| 86ème | Apollinaire |
| 94ème | Gertrude Stein |
| 96ème | Modigliani |
| 97ème | Piaf |
| | Eluard |

We could see right away how
iron was an ill-advised

substance for crypt doors
in the 19th century

Some of them
        had slit-like windows
                in the shapes of crosses

so that you could look within
upon a tiny room with
an altar   a vase   a statue of Mary
        with flowers long dried
                to a ring of dust
        & a stained glass window
                to the rear

often there were low-built chairs
with kneeling cushions
                just above the floor
for the grown-up middle class
                to pray for their parents

now so dirty and chaotic
no one had knelt
        for half a hundred


I push my eyebrow
                to the cross
and stare in the gloom
and spot upon
        the prayer chair
                an object
                        almost gleaming

a packet
of spaghetti gum!


I searched for the grave
of the socialist singer

Béranger

at whose funeral once
a mighty crowd
            lined the boulevards

Not many seek
        out the socialist
                    song-crafter

on his iron street
of rust and toppled stone

but I know
        the
            dream
                seeps
through the rust.


I think of his beautiful trees
at the bronze statue of
Corot
        on a wall
    above a raspberry bush
        leaking green
down its stony pediment.

Miriam notes how everywhere you look—
at the roots
        shoving aside the
                            gray

the vandalized stain glass

the rusting crypt locks

    the Sprite cans
        shining in th'
            taphic darkness

you realize
what an Ozymandias
scene it is.


We found the taph of Frédéric Chopin

a white marble lady
melted in the acid rain
her head bent down in grief
holding a pitted babylonian lyre

Someone has clipped off
her left foretoe
& pried off her 4th finger
which has now just a protruding
iron rivet wire

a clutch of
roses
        tucked
into the wrought-iron fence
with F.C. scrolled
                in iron
too
    across the bars

& I thought of
those quick white fingers
in front of the piano
            that afternoon
playing the Ocean Étude

because isn't that what
it's all about—

        the Ocean Étude

the cool lizard slides
down the torso of Ozymandias

     it's the Ocean Étude

the magpie in the acacia
   flaps away from Colette

     in the Ocean Étude

Nature loves to hide itself
   till it's time for the
      marble fingers to play

     the Ocean Étude

The spikey rod
   where once the finger stood
     conducts

     the Ocean Étude

We search for Morrison
   along these dusty quais & bone bins

Others also seek
    You can see them walking
        with a Perrier or wine
      across the thanatopolis

guided by hand-drawn signs
    JIM

        JIM

            JIM

I spot the writing 50 feet away

    JIM MORRISON
    1943–1971

A statue of his head and shoulders
on a rough-hewn block of stone

The left side of his nose seems smashed away
and someone has peace-signed
      the final O of his name.

Every nearby family crypt is covered—
very covered, with 1000s of messages
You can see they've painted them
        over with slip
as if they were NY subway cars
They must have done it year after year.

All these hasty taph-graphs
    these bright magic markers
      these hieroglyphics of fandom

give me a feeling of funerary Egypt,
of the Theban necropolis,

of some jittery-handed *Book of the Dead*
on a outdoor tablature

"HALLUCINATIONS"
writ in
magenta marker
just above
the words
(carved in stone)
"CONCESSION A PERPETUITE"

& below
it a large
spray-painted
red

on the back of a tomb topped with
a cross arising from drapings

I walk around the back to
read the names & dates

ICI REPOSENT
J. L. BRUNEL
11-9-1814
4-4-1855

Big red letters

# GLORIA

on the
Famille du Thorel

TIME TO LIVE
TIME TO CRY
TIME TO LAUGH
TIME TO DIE
TAKE IT EASY BABE
TAKE IT AS IT COMES

Hey Jimey Jim
See you in the
dark of LA
tonight

**LSD**

on a tall crypt-wall

Before I sink
into the big sleep

Jim always drank
at Pepo's

I want to
hear the scream of
the butterfly

Blood/ is the rose/
of mysterious/ union

All Hail
the American Knight

Come back, Jim

Jim, why did you
have to leave so soon?

Rock & Roll
Heaven

Jimi Hendrix
Jim Morrison
John Lennon
Janis Joplin

Successful Hills are here to stay

graff' after graff'
and hundreds, maybe thousands
just leaving their
names or initials
and also on the insides of
tombs whose doors have
been pulled open

A rusty iron gate
yanked off and
                set inside

the vaulted room

        with
        red

FREEDOM FOR CROATIA

near the apex of the vault.


I can't decide
        what all this says
                about the human condition

but there is something
        eerily beautiful
                about his face

in this
        loony Egyptian garden

where each day they set
                offerings around the bust

So far today some yellow roses
                        in a Heineken bottle
some brandy, a vase, a pot of living geraniums
some bottle caps, greeting cards, a poem

and to the side, tucked behind
someone else's stone
a pile of yesterday's offerings

limp blossoms, wine, coca-cola, orange
slices, cognac bottles.


We notice the dirt
        beneath his stone
Somehow
        it seemed disturbed
without a granite slab
                        above it.

Miriam agreed.
        "I wouldn't want
        to bet my life
        Morrison's in there

        —and how
        long was he in there
        about a week?"

she said,
as we walked
down the cobbles
                out of the 6th Division

I recalled that spring of '68
The Fugs were playing the Avalon Ballroom
A band called Joy of Cooking
                    was singing
You were in our dressing room
dressed in some sort of
lizard skin or snake skin trousers

frail and curly
holding a Jack Daniels bottle
like some Bacchus-Orpheus splice.

That is the image I have of you
Jim Morrison
who went for the risks
        on the spiral staircase
                where a lot of the poets
                        stand & sway, tremble
                        & stumble, tumble & fall.

        So long, lizard legs
        I said
        as we walked
                up the hill
        to leave a little book of verse
                by the tall stone
                        of Apollinaire

                              —May 1987

# Rothschild's Fiddle

*—adapted from a story by Anton Chekhov*


It was a small town
filled with old people who rarely passed away
and Yakov the coffin maker
had little business
He lived in a one-room cabin
with Marfa his wife
a stove, a stack of coffins,
a carpenter's bench, a bed plus cooking utensils.

Yakov was tall and stout and seventy
He made his well-joined coffins stout like he,
all of a size, modeled on himself.

He also played fiddle at weddings
with a Jewish orchestra.
He was very skillful at Russian songs
Yakov had grown anti-Semitic for no good reason
over the years
especially at the playing of the fluteplayer Rothschild
Yakov yelled at the band leader
and was rarely hired after that

The coffin business, as we have said, was scanty
& Yakov waited impatiently for sick people to worsen
Sometimes a sick person would pass away elsewhere
and he would tally up the money he had lost
and pull out his fiddle late at night
to play a sad, dirgy tune

    (violin melody)

Then his wife Marfa suddenly was ill

"Yakov, I am dying," Marfa said.

For fifty-two years they were married yet
Yakov had never rubbed her sore back
or given caresses during the long nights
sleeping by the stove

He'd never paid any attention to her
any more than if she were
a cat or dog by the house
nor given her any presents
and thought he might now get her one
but it was too late.

Never bought her a winter kerchief
never brought her cake from any of the weddings
but oh-so-often rushed at her with fists
and when he lost a coffin-making job
he blamed her
and because he didn't want to spend the money on tea
she drank hot water in the mornings

He took her in a neighbor's cart to the hospital
where Yakov was glad they had only to wait
for three hours

The doctor would not see them
so the assistant looked at Marfa

"She seems to have influenza and some fever," he said
"Typhus has also come to the town.

How old is your wife?"

"Sixty-nine"

"She's an old woman. Maybe it's time."

Yakov bowed and replied, "Thank you for your
remarks, but you know, every insect is fond of life"

The doorman said "I will tell you what to do.

Put a cold compress on her head, and have
her take these powders twice a day.
Now good-bye"

When they returned to the cabin
Marfa was unsteady and held onto the stove
She was afraid to lie down
lest Yakov shout she was lazy
and doing no work

Yakov knew he would soon have to
build a coffin
and so went to his wife and measured her

after which she lay down
Yakov made the sign of the cross
then began to saw and nail

When he was done, he put on his reading glasses
and entered into his book of losses
"Marfa Ivanovna's coffin—two rubles and 40 kopecks"

Toward nightfall, she called out to Yakov
"Do you remember, Yakov"

she had a face of joy as she looked over at her husband
"remember how fifty years ago great God
gave us a baby with yellow hair. You and I, o my Yakov,
used to go down to the river every day with the baby
and sit under the willow tree and sing songs."

Then Marfa laughed with utmost bitterness.
She said, "the baby died."

"That's just your imagination," was all that Yakov could
think of replying
              in this most ultimate of talks

Later that night the priest came

and just before dawn Marfa Ivanovna
                              returned to starlight

The women of nearby houses
washed her and wrapped her in winding sheets
Four men carried the coffin to the graveyard
followed by a cortege of old women,
beggars, and two cripples

He admired how well he had made the coffin
as he said good-bye to Marfa
                          for the final time

Yakov felt so weary walking back home.
He sat in the cabin
regretting his neglect and disrespect
of his wife
all the years of angry toil
the scrimping when yet
            enough was there to help ease pain

Suddenly, the man named Rothschild
from the village band
came to the door,

"There's a big wedding on the weekend"

Yakov spumed with hostility
"Get out of here! I have no peace with Jews!"
he shouted

Rothschild replied, "You'd better be more
polite, or I will toss you over the fence."

Then Yakov made fists and rushed at Rothschild
and Rothschild
        ran for his life

As he hastened away

boys in nearby houses
ran after him, chanting "Jew, Jew, Jew . . ."

Later that day Yakov walked the path by the river's edge
He looked to the other shore
and noticed that the big birch forest had been chopped down
and he saw the thick ancient willow tree
with a huge hollow and a raven's nest
when suddenly he remembered the child with the
yellow hair Marfa had mentioned

Ahh, it was the same willow. How old it now was!
Ahh, why had they cut down the beautiful birches
                    from 50 years ago?
He wondered why he had rushed at Rothschild
                    as if to beat him up
And why had fate brought him to the making of coffins
And why did not people
                    ease each other's suffering in peace?


That night Yakov's sleep was full of dreams
He saw Marfa, the willow tree, the river,
the cut down birches, and the sad face of Rothschild.
He arose several times in the night to play the violin

        (short violin melody)

Yakov awakened ill and trembling
then walked to the hospital
where they gave him useless compresses
He knew his life was almost done

He was not sad to die
but wondered what would happen to his beautiful fiddle

Everything was doomed
just like the birch and pine forest
everything would ooze into decay

Back at home he sat on the door sill
then lifted up his fiddle and
began to play
with the tears rolling down from his eyes
the sad rolling mourning of final times

While he was playing Rothschild approached
opened the gate latch
spotted Yakov in the doorway,
and turned as if to run away

"Come on in, don't be afraid," said Yakov
with a friendly voice

Rothschild said, "I apologize for bothering
you, but the band leader has sent me.
There's a big wedding coming up in town
and he begs you to join us"

"I cannot go," said Yakov. "I am ill, brother."

Then he began playing again
Rothschild listened closely
and became engrossed in the suffering and grief
in Yakov's melody.

He rolled his eye, and exclaimed "wacchchch,"
and Rothschild's tears made dark splotches
                              on his green frock coat.

"Give the fiddle to Rothschild," Yakov
told the priest
just before his final sleep.

Later those in the town wondered with marvel
how Rothschild acquired such a treasure

He no longer played the flute
and when he performed the violin tune he'd learned

from Yakov, the audience always wept.

This new song was so well-liked in the town
the wealthy merchants and public officials always
hired Rothschild for their parties and events,
and sometimes he was forced to play
the melody ten times or more.

## The Close of My Lecture at the
## Rock & Roll Hall of Fame & Museum


INTRODUCTION: I was invited to give a talk, with music, at the Rock & Roll Hall of Fame and Museum on the music scene in the 1960s in New York City. I focused on the music of the Civil Rights movement, folk rock, psychedelic music, and on songwriters such as Phil Ochs, John Sebastian, and those who wrote in the Brill Building, life for musicians in Greenwich Village and the Lower East Side, and the rise of recording technology.

You recall the last
time you saw someone

a conversation
a flash of color
the sound of a table scraping
& then they're gone

Or you say good-bye
to an era
a year
a book
a poem you'll never read again

or maybe you'll reread it
again & again
or think about it
        as long as thoughts
keep flowing through
the circuits of your brain

        The vestiges
        remain in the time-track

        some songs, some tapes,
        some posters,
            some diaries
        some memories of kisses
        & kudos

and then we are gone.

# By the Mona Lisa Lyre

*(an electronic music instrument)*
*as I begin writing* America, a History in Verse

Oh how imperfect am I
confused earthling     Edward Sanders

at age 58!

Reading many books about
                the history of America

scared, sore-backed
                fearful of decay
& still determined
            to go out
                in a blaze of leaflets

To my right
        a musical device

        built into the Mona Lisa

& leftward
     leftward
the entire story of the
          miracle of the rose

# Thirsting for Peace in a Raging Century

### I.

I'm thirsting for peace in a raging century
Thirsting for peace in a raging century

I called on the Universe to scroll me some answers
but the Universe, it wreaks, but rarely speaks

> O scroll me
> some answers
> o Universe
> Tell me if
> anyone wakes up
> when the hieroglyphs sing

> Just tell me yes or no

*I'm thirsting for peace in a raging century*
*Thirsting for peace in a raging century*

### 2.

> Scroll me some glyphs
> o Sky
> like the living
> papyrus rolls
> they placed
> in the coffins of Thebes
>         3,000 years ago

> They stunned my youth
> I'd had so few full moments of joy
> till my eye-brain flowed joy in the Scrolls

> that told of the long, scrolly walk
> on paths of papyrus so hot they scorched the feet

past hawk-headed gods &
scary spiritual assessors
past lakes of fire
past moments of Mystes
& torches stubbed out
          in pails of milk

then judgement
up against the Feather of Justice
          on the scales of eternity

It stunned my youth
I'd had so few full moments of joy
to know they had actually believed
the words and pictures were alive
to make a safe footpath
for the dead dancer Her-Weben
          down near the damp heat of Isis

No greater belief in
words has there been

*I'm thirsting for peace in a raging century*
*Thirsting for peace in a raging century*

3.

## The Soap Clay

When I was 12
I used to walk with friends
to the old stone ruins
of a pioneer house
at the top of Soap Clay Cliff

Not far from where the Younger outlaw gang
            carved their names
                        on an outlaw tree

I hunger for the soap clay
the pioneers used
in the bend of the creek

to wash on their
way to picket fences
& houses on the sod

I wish they could have washed
                        their meanness out
& made their mean times end
            on Soap Clay bend

*I'm thirsting for peace in a raging century*
*Thirsting for peace in a raging century*

4.

## The Feather of Justice

I believe in the Feather of Justice
The Egyptians
called it the Maat Feather
It's  light
    It's perfect
        It belongs to eternity

I believe
in the feather of Justice

It measures our lives
        in the World of Forms

It calls the evil
        away from the good

It's in our cells
It's in the path of the sun

& sometimes the universe
cuts the Feather
        to make a pen
               for the bard

I believe in the Feather of Justice
*La Plume Égyptian*

*I'm thirsting for peace in a raging century*
*Thirsting for peace in a raging century*

The dark gray slate
is cracking
        with taphic frost heave!

Splitting
in two across the
top, & working down
            only about a third of the
            way so far,

so that the writing
is unaffected

I sketch
    it quickly
        & Miriam
    hands me a
    black sea crow
            feather

*I'm thirsting for peace in a raging century*
*Thirsting for peace in a raging century*

6.

Spiritual Topography

Blend your spirit
into the
rush
    of your river

Let the
whirls of your brain
fit in with
the contours
    of the ground you love

for
when the curves
of your spirit
flow out to embrace
the curves of the land

That's love
That's habitat
That's the kissing of landforms
                with your soul

*I'm thirsting for peace in a raging century*
*Thirsting for peace in a raging century*

## 7.

I read in a book
that the universe may well have
ten dimensions (at least!)
Some days I hear
the songs of moms
    and tio-tio-ing birds
in all of them
and does not the universe play
Blake's "Laughing Song"
              at least once a year?
I can hear you, Klebnikov
I can hear you, Blake
I can hear you, Hawking

Just taking the time
to read this poem
    adds to the overall chaos
Stephen Hawking says.

First there's yes    Then there's no
Then combinations of yes and no
Then it's like a brew:
    7 parts yes one part no
    3 parts no one part yes
yes-yes-yes-no-no   no-no-no-yes-yes
Why is why whying? Mr. Einstein
Why is why whying? Mr. Hawking

*I'm thirsting for peace in a raging century*
*Thirsting for peace in a raging century*

8.
The Rinse of Nonsense

The vowels are in the air!
        hey nonny hee!
The consonants are drumming!
        ho nonny free!
I'm laughing with glee-dare!
        hie nonny be!
I'm laughing with Blake's summer pen
Laughing & laughing & laughing
Klob! Kooma! Kafto!
Laughing & laughing & laughing
Kreeb! Krobe! Krybe! Krube!

I'm taking a long hot shower
        like a million years
                in the rinse of nonsense
& I can feel all the thrills in its heaven

*I'm thirsting for peace in a raging century*
*Thirsting for peace in a raging century*


9.

I know that peace is a quick, temporary fragment
It's not enough to heal & be contrite
nor read through all the wisdom

yet we must shape a window
                with the shards of our lives

        I wanted peace
        I wanted the wall of peace
        I wanted to go all
                the way on the golden thread
        I wanted it
        I broke my knuckles
                scraping at the wall

& I wanted at last to drink
  from the waters of stillness
but the waters are afire with oil
It chars my lips
  but still I keep drinking

*I'm thirsting for peace in a raging century*
*Thirsting for peace in a raging century*


10.


I see the Final Leaflet
It's blazing on the hillside
Its letters are straight and perfect

& it speaks of a world
where everything is done
  to ease the pain of living

I'm going out in a blaze of leaflets

1789   1825   1848   1870   1905
1918   1968   2008
every few decades
  another surge
    to ease the pain of living

*I'm thirsting for peace in a raging century*
*Thirsting for peace in a raging century*


11.


I think of Sappho often
Her life on little tattered papyrus shreds
or snippets in critics—
Longinus, or Dionysius of Halicarnassus

I love her songs of longing

—the one in the meters known as
the 2nd paean, and Ionic a majore

Something like:
Selanna (the moon) has dipped
and the Pleiades too
Ah midnight darkens
           & I sleep alone . . .

but, you know, there's so much more
in her sequences of sound

O Sappho! Sappho!
Shreds! Shreds!

They heated the baths
          with your verse
and I think of you every day

*I'm thirsting for peace in a raging century*
*Thirsting for peace in a raging century*

## 12

### Rock & Roll and Roll Away the Rock

Uespere autem sabbati, quae lucescit in prima sabbati, venit
Maria Magdalene, et altera Maria videre sepulchrum. Et ecce
terrae motus factus est magnus. Angelus enim Domini
descendit de caelo: et accedens revoluit lapidem, et sedebat
super eum. Erat autem aspectus eius sicut fulgur: et
vestimentum eius sicut nix. Prae timore autem eius exterriti
sunt custodes, et facti sunt velut mortui. Respondens autem
angelus dixit mulieribus: Nolite timere uos: scio enim, quod
Iesum, qui crucifixus est, quaeritis. Non est hic, surrexit enim,
sicus dixit: venite, videte locum, ubi positus erat Dominus.
*Matthew* 28:1

Three days later
the two sad Marys came to the cave
& the ground began to quake
and an angel descended from the sky
and rolled away the rock

His face was like lightning
his clothing like snow
Rock and roll and roll away the rock

Do not be afraid, he said
for I know that you seek Jesus
He is not here, for he is arisen
Come and see the place where
              the Lord lay
Rock and roll and roll away the rock
rock and roll and roll away the rock

*I'm thirsting for peace in a raging century*
*Thirsting for peace in a raging century*

13.

Pindar sang that "Water is the greatest thing"
That's how he began his
        "First Olympian Ode"
and it will not be enough
till the poisons are gone
from the nectar
        the hummingbird licks
                from the swamp flowers


*I'm thirsting for peace in a raging century*
*Thirsting for peace in a raging century*


                14.

        Late at night
        frail
                w/ sleep sloth
        the burdens
        & mistakes
        seem so overwhelming

        things undone,  things ill done
        the blunders

        till the
        famous fingers of sleep
        rub your soul
        rolf your vim
        kiss your trauma
        heal your vastness

        and morning
        brings a crack of grace
                        again

*I'm thirsting for peace in a raging century*
*Thirsting for peace in a raging century*

15.

I believe in the healing of the windows
I am healed in Matisse's blue
I am healed in the color plates of Goethe
I am healed in the hues of John Scotus Erigena
I lift my face upon the splintered windows
                                    to be healed

Someone has placed the mallow rose
in a perfect window
        shaped like a wheat-loaf
See my shadow on the other side
See my shadow on the other side

*I'm thirsting for peace in a raging century*
*Thirsting for peace in a raging century*

# Stolen Elections

*—a Chant in A Minor—*

*—After researching the elections of 2000, 2002, and 2004 for seven years, and filling up a couple of bankers boxes with files, here's what I think happened.*

The far right wing hates a paper trail
It loves computers that lose your mail:
"The Constitution's not a suicide note
So please don't complain about a crooked vote"
*Stolen Elections*

The right wing owns so many of the papers
The right wing controls the television scrapers
It's the only thing left for them to steal—
to lock up the voting in a right wing wheel
*Stolen Elections*

### Clinton Era

The right wing saw how Clinton clung to power
when Monica's knee-pads couldn't hurl him from the tower

So the right wing growled, "If they won't vote right,
then we'll have to rig the count in the vote-rig night!
*Stolen Elections*

"We'll never let it happen" the right wing gloats
"Change a few computer chips, before it floats!
Control the computers you control the votes!
Listen to their mewly moans, the left-wing shoats!"
*Stolen Elections*

### Gore

They flew down to Florida to stop the count
Republican goons like a machine gun mount

It was worse than Watergate    It was treason sublime
The way they jimmied Florida with their right wing slime
        *Stolen Election*

### 2002

After Wellstone's plane was maybe shot dead
Walter Mondale was comfortably ahead
On election day the polls were way wrong
& the voting computers sang a right-wing song
        *Stolen Election*

Down in Georgia Max Cleland gonna win
Ahead in the polls with voting to begin
It was more than a mystery when he lost that night
No paper trail to check if they got it right
        *Stolen Election*

### 2004

Kerry looked good in 2 thousand 4
All the exit polls showed "Bush on the floor"
But then some computers in Ohio start to click
They rearranged some numbers to make Bush stick
        *Stolen election*

It's as bad as Pearl Harbor    Bad as Bunker Hill
the Constitution laid out for a kill
Some feel an evil to falsify the run
They say the Bill of Rights's not a suicide gun
        *Stolen Elections*

### 2010

So, come on, Americans, stand up for the Vote
or you may have a tyrant  in a skull-filled boat
America's in danger from a right-wing pox
but you can stop it sharp w/ an honest Ballot Box
        *& Honest Elections*

## Jefferson, Hamilton, Kennedy, Cheney

Jefferson was convinced that
Hamilton was a crook
but if he was
he got away with it

Some are convinced
that they "let it happen"
I wouldn't put it past Cheney
but it's going to be
              difficult to prove

Take Operation Northwoods
                   back in '62
This one is pretty well proven:

The u.s. Joint Chiefs of Staff
(chaired by the right-wing general named Lyman Lemnitzer)
sent a proposal to JFK to set up Operation Northwoods
to "develop a Communist Cuban terror campaign
in the Miami area
     . . . and even in Washington"

in order to rouse the u.s. populace
                   to an ire-fire of anger—

"We could blow up a u.s. ship in Guantanamo Bay
              and blame Cuba"
         wrote the Chiefs

"Casualty lists in u.s. newspapers
would cause a helpful wave of indignation."

The Chiefs also recommended "exploding a few plastic bombs
in carefully chosen spots, the arrest of Cuban agents
and the release of prepared documents
                   substantiating Cuban involvement . . ."

The u.s. Joint Chiefs also proposed
to blow up an empty drone plane
      disguised as a commercial flight
                              & blame the Cubans:

"An aircraft at Elgin AFB would be painted and numbered as
an exact duplicate for a civil registered aircraft belonging to a CIA
proprietary organization in the Miami area. At a designated time
the duplicate would be substituted for the actual civil aircraft
and would be loaded with the selected passengers, all boarded
under carefully prepared aliases. The actual registered
aircraft would be converted to a drone (a remotely controlled
unmanned aircraft). Take off times of the drone aircraft and the
actual aircraft will be scheduled to allow a rendezvous south of
Florida." The drone would be exploded over Cuba
and then Castro accused of killing an innocent group
                                            of Americans.

(Kennedy rejected the plan in March of '62)

          Jefferson was convinced that
          Hamilton was a crook
          but if he was
          it never inked a book

# The "Jumping" Landmine

Some mines leap up
from the ground
like ghouls in a graveyard


then blast the child's eyes blind
in the fields of evil

# In the Spring of 1968 I Drew a Glyph

for the Fugs album liner notes
& there it is
　　38 years later
　　　　in the archives.


2006

## The Ultimate Landfill

All that American stuff
sliding from the end of the
      Big Chicken Foot

down into the depths
off the Continental Shelf

———————————————

"Because the bird-foot delta has grown so far into the gulf . . . the river's mouth
is at the edge of the Continental shelf. As a result the (120 million tons per
year of) sediment it carries ends up in deep water, where it is lost forever."
—*The New York Times,* September 10, 2006

## My Political Causes Are Hopeless


My political causes are hopeless
Iceland is polluting itself
Governments are privatizing
in cunningness

yet the goal is the same for the privatizers—
a vast underculture of early death
            & jails

and the good folk
        get to die broke & weeping.

But you're making it much too simple—

Social democracy shall prevail
but the laurels your sort will wear
                Eddie boy

will be genetically modified
to sport the colors of
the official souvenir book of the
NASCAR Global Warming 500

# The View
# of Centuries

# Quick Black Hole Spin-Change

I don't like it—

two massive Black Holes
each twirling at the core of
                two merging galaxies

get close enough
to fuse together

then quick as a wink
just as they are melting into a New Black Hole Blob

they undergo something called a "spin-flip"

they change the axes of their spins
and the fused-together Black Hole Blob
gets its own
                quick as a cricket's foot

Don't like it at all

And then the new Black Hole Blob sometimes
bounces back and forth inside
                its mergèd Galaxy

till it settles at the center

but sometimes a "newly" up-sized Black Hole
leaves its Galaxy
to sail out munchingly on its own
                into the Universal It

I don't like it

Nothing about it
in the Bhagavad Gita
the Book of Revelation
Shakespeare, Sappho, or Allen Ginsberg

# Elegy

Gil Gil
   Paul Paul
      Joel Joel
         gone gone

# The Brain Boat

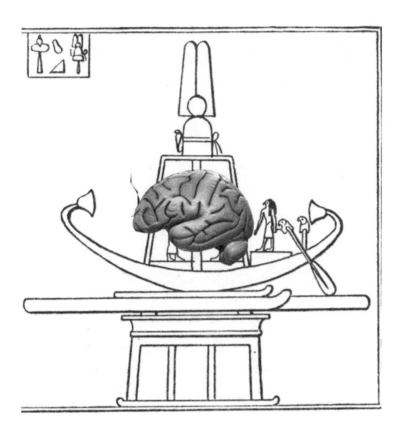

The Brain Boat
sails in the vastness

## A Narcissus on the Lawn on Mother's Day

Light-yellow on the outside
egg yolky within
the Narcissus
blooms for weeks
beneath the euonymous

o how I wish my mother
had bloomed more & more

on Cemetery Hill
this Mother's Day

She'd be just 103!
& in a senior assisted living place

o Mither Mollie
woman of the Ozarks
& of the limestone layers
          of the Missouri sea!

How I wish you were here
still playing bridge
          with Marge Quinn
& 15 card tables full of women laughing

## Standing with Larry Faeth on Cemetery Hill

He was my best friend in high school

He drove me to the cemetery
to trim the hedges to the left and right
of my parents' grave

He helped me pull out several vines
that were protruding from the hedge tops

and then we walked over to his parents' grave
His mom had passed away not long ago

and there was a fresh sadness to his voice

Next he drove me to the house he had bought and
refurbished for her final years

showed me the addition he had built
to give her plants and flowers more space and better light

It was empty now. I could feel he wanted to weep
when he talked of the auction of her furniture
held not long ago. He pointed to the steps
where the auctioneer stood

All our moms and dads, and soon we ourselves
in the long charity of time.

## Missing the Boat

So many worried about missing the boat
or having it overturned

in their dusty sequences, books,  their *cursus honorum*

so & so got a MacArthur
such & so was accepted by Allen
such & when had a thicker scrapbook than F. Scott Fitzgerald!
then & why had 400 letters from Beckett

worried about leaving their livers in Peoria
their life-long love on Loser Row
their wet poems in a wet jacket on a wet sea

all of them, however howling or honed to regret
manage to keep afloat

in their

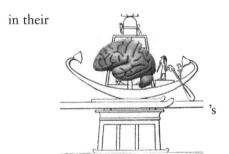

's

till, you know, that Bergman moment

The Scythester

after which it's all archaeology
and the judgements of the studious

—Christmas Morn, 2007

## The Resilience of Heh Heh


Heh heh
makes itself known

Heh heh

throughout history
all the way back

Heh heh

to hungry torch-men

Heh

roaming in the creeks

Heh heh

of melting glaciers

Heh Heh

92 centuries
in front of Wm Blake's
             "Laughing Song"

## Let's Not Keep Fighting the Trojan War


Simone Weil took a train to the front
when the Civil War began in the summer of '36

She joined the ranks of an Anarchist Unit
and picked up a rifle though never fired

She suffered an injury, not from a bullet
and her parents came to her rescue

She'd been taken aback by the violence
her own side had committed

and soon published an essay
"Ne recommençons pas la guerre de Troie"

which I have slightly changed to
"Let's Not Keep Fighting the Trojan War"

especially now that the Air Force is insisting
on designing all-terrain cluster bombs
able to crawl and hop for miles
                              in search of a victim

## A Visit to Jack's Memorial Park

I walk among the canals of the Merrimac
& also past the lithe-limbed statue that honors the women
who let's face it slaved in the mills

till I came upon Jack's little memorial park
on Bridge Street. Skrunk! Skrunk! Skrunk!
It was filled with skateboarders! in the Catholic afternoon
near the shiny green bridge across the River

Rest in Pacem oh writer of Lowell
in your checkerboard coat
in the nervous elevator
up to the Buckley show
late in life, sipping your whiskey
from a little bottle, in between rounds of talk

"Life spills out," as Olson says
and so it does as the boys skrunk happily
among your tall shiny stones, o Jack Kerouac

where I catch in a blaze your sense of
being part of eternity
staring at your writings carved in the shiny

I am feeling the awe of the Loner commingling
so Newly
amidst all the conservatism

O Jack, phantom of the Lonely Dream
Daimon of the skrunks!
Silly Boy with a right-wing mom
& her vehement love
Apostle of the Holy Ghost beneath the Bodhi Tree

it's a peaceful afternoon, and all is not lost
thanks to your neat sense of yourself as a lonely American genius

    —in Lowell for the Massachusetts Poetry Festival
    October 2008

## Ode to the Beat Generation

*—for Antonio Bertoli*


Hail to the Beat Generation in the Time-Mist!
Hail to the Generation that rocked across the ocean
with a mighty Boat of Books that shook all cities!

*Beat Beat Beat Beat*

Thank God for cameras, o Beat Generation
for they have captured your wild dance forever!
Thank God for mimeograph machines & inexpensive presses
for they have inked your Final Type!
Thank God for the angels in your canvases, O Generation!
And may the candles in your Chianti bottles light up heaven, o Beats,
and no one ever publish hell again!
Thank God for your Beautiful Loss, o Beat Generation
Thank God for the concept of "Gone"!
They can't extinguish Gone, no matter how hard they try!
Sacred Gone! Eternal Gone! Fishin' Gone!

*Beata Beatus Beatum Beatae*

They can't extinguish the flames of your sandals, O Beat Generation!
and the Egyptian kohl that outlines your wanton eyes!
They can't extinguish the bongo drums
at midnight on the Staten Island Ferry
in the Waters of Gone!
nor the crevices and wild appendages insatiate
from Moscow to Moravia to Memphis!

*Beat-Gone Beat-Begone Beat-Gone Beat-Begone*

The strands of time are like a baklava, o Beat Generation!
So many layers, and laughs, and lines, and Lones!
Creeley typing the stencils for the mimeographed "Howl"
on Rexroth's typewriter!

Ferlinghetti's left-wing poems of people tired of repairing
        Ezekiel's wheel for a shot of whiskey!
di Prima typing "Revolution" across the dead eyes of tyrants!
The dueling economies of Burroughs and Ginsberg!
The broccoli swords of Corso and Gary Snyder!
The knowledge of the 1,000 year sigh in Joanne Kyger's genius!

   *Beat-Brain Beat-Brine Beat-Brawn Beat-Boat*

I'm not going to talk about your weaknesses
in the River of Kiss-Phantoms, o Beat Generation!
Nor talk about Kerouac's voting for Nixon one nervous November
nor speak of the cash-starved notebooks of flip-out
in somebody's archive, or the fields of stunned Sunflowers
surrounded by so many suns
they turn to the actual Sun of Gone
to find Eternity!

   *Beat Beat Beat Beat*

The art of the Road and the art of the Word is the art of the Rose
We hear you! o Beat Generation, down by the sunny marsh
singing for 60 years like the frogs of Aristophanes:
        Ecstasy Fondue! Sax Clover! Tire-Sandal Soup!

   *Beat Beat Beat Beat*
   *Never a sheet so sweet!*

## Amram

If Kerouac had lived
would Amram's good will
have turned him into
a Democrat?

# The Socialism of Carl Sandburg

1878–1967

Let's face it, the loud-mouthed
        threats of rightist agitators
                pulled Sandburg away from his politics

that, and the exigencies of working for the mass media
which ever draggeth its writers from socialism

plus the labors of factional friction
waiting to speak at lonely meetings
and the endless arguments of the Left

Son of Swedish immigrants

part of the Truth of the Upper Midwest

at nineteen did the hobo
        to the West, labored in wheatfields and hotels

Had a way with words,
worked through Lombard College
                selling stereoscopic pictures

first book *In Reckless Ecstasy*    Nov 1904

began writing on labor

gave several lectures on Whitman

active in Wisconsin Social-Democratic Party politics, 1907–'12

found a strength at
                rousing a public crowd

1908 married Lilian Steichen
                socialist intellectual

In '08 Sandburg campaigned with Debs
        on the Red Special tour of Wisconsin, introducing Debs in
        Appleton, where Carl & Lilian were living

He discovered the guitar!
began to chant and sing
            some of his poems

Spring o' '10 Sandburg was secretary to the socialist mayor of Milwaukee

He wrote widely-disseminated socialist tracts
                            for various pubs

1912 moved to Chi
still unknown as po

Chicago poems published '14 in *Poetry*

and he slowly oozed away from overt socialism
                        toward earning a living from ink

(even though we know that "the Secret Mind whispers")

*Cornhuskers* a book in 1918 gave him po-fame

In '20s worked on Abe Lincoln bio in multi-vol

    In 1927
            his *American Songbag*

        pulsing                    the secret mind
        through                    song-work

1940 Pulitzer for history

'40 he worked with Dorothy Parker and Helen Keller to
"help the American Rescue Ship Mission transport Spanish refugees
from France to Mexico to save them from Hitler and Franco"
(in the words of the *Encylopedia of the American Left*)

They moved to Flat Rock, NC
where Lilian raised prize goats

1951 his second Pulitzer for *Complete Poems*

Died in July of 1967 at eighty-nine

Lyndon Johnson spoke at a service for him
    at the Lincoln Memorial
    where Lincoln was whispering
    the Secret Mind was Whispering

    and every banjo carries the tune

# Long View

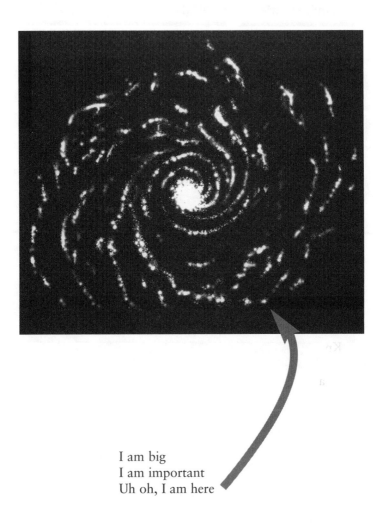

I am big
I am important
Uh oh, I am here

# Hölderlin's Tower

Once by the Neckar
I stood next to Hölderlin's Tower
there like a Greek myth
as an example

& fed the swans.

Pitch a tent among stones
and practice your recitations
in the cistern of the muses.

Crises?
Caught balling?
Fled Frankfurt
Flipped.

Uh oh: "alternate depression
              and nervous irritability"

Knew Greek
    translated *Antigone* and *Oedipus Rex*
    and nine odes of Pindar

bonk bonk

to Tübingen in the
summer of 1807
harmlessly bonk

Lived in the Tower till
permaGaia June 7, 1843.

Friedrich Friedrich
stay in your Tower

The good folk of Tübingen
still mention your sadness

They point to your house
as if you were still there
even though it's been a century more
since your lungs pulled in air

Gontard may have felt he was balling his wife
May have caught them kissing, smoky with strife

There were angry words, and the poet was fired
And life wended onward, hopeless and mired

Hölderlin, Hölderlin kiss your love in quickness
Now and then, quick meetings, as if eros were a sickness

Did they fuck? Nothing in ink has survived
It doesn't matter much now, just sorrow contrived

More and more crazy, in loveless ups and downs
Looking for tutoring jobs in poetless towns

Till he learned Susette died from measles one summer
And all of the future was the moan of a mummer

He wended even more be-bonked, aft' he lost his Susette
He wandered back to Tübingen with naught but regret

When a well-to-do cabinet maker named Ernst Zimmer
Who was reading his novel *Hyperion*, gave him a glimmer

Invited him to dwell in that tall yellow Tower
Food, solace, and comradeship, for poetry's flower

Sometimes he was out, sometimes in
Sometimes the Universe has a clownface grin

Writhing in sadness, 'spersed with gladness
For when a person truly knows, they call it madness

Look at the world
So caustic and cruel
poet v. poet, drool for a duel

It's tempting to hide
away from such fuel

A few lines when calm enough
and the seas not so rough

Sometimes I pray
for an endless hour
living in the upper
of Hölderlin's tower

I'd stroll from the yellow
in my snowtime scarf
with crumbs for the swans
from the Crazy Man's wharf

## Lists

I wrote Galway Kinnell to ask him to send a verse for
The New Amazing Grace
He wrote back quite friendly
that he "seemed to live from deadline to deadline"
& did not have the time.

It's the same right here on Meads Mountain Road:
I'm overwhelmed with details!
There's literally a thousand things to do each minute!
And my ever-whitening head
leans down close to the white-paged clipboard
darkened with the ravens of list-quoth!

I'm trying to think of some answers
The end will come some day
& there will be
          the unfulfilled clipboard
                    of Eternity
resting on my desk.

Not even a billion parallel universes
where I'm holding
a blackened clipboard in each
would be enough
          to list what needs to be done

There are no laurels
There is no rest
There are only lists!

## Hymn to Unpremeditated Goof

I want to go back to the golden days
    of   Goof   Goof   Goof   Goofitude
      Goof   Goof   Goof   Goofitude

Read a book       Listen to a record
Working on a painting   at the very same time
    Goof   Goof   Goof
    Goof   Goof   Goof

Unpremeditated
    Unpreprogrammed
      Unregimented
          Goofitude!
    Goof   Goof   Goofitude

I want to go back to the days
When we lived in a purple haze
Dancing on the head of a bobby pin
Happy in the body  like a crazy grin
    Goof   Goof   Goof
    Goof   Goof   Goof

We were beating on our drums in a midnight glow
While you read your poems to an overflow
When the time came up for the sax to blow
All of us were shouting  Go! Go! Go!
    Goof   Goof   Goof
    Goof   Goof   Goof

Take me back to those golden days
    of   Goof   Goof  Goof  Goofitude
      Goof   Goof  Goof  Goofitude

Build a dome       stare at the creek
Take a vacation for 25 weeks
    Goof   Goof   Goof

           Goof    Goof    Goof

Unpremeditated
        Unpreprogrammed
                Unregimented
                            Goofitude!
        Goof    Goof    Goof
        Gone    Gone    Gone
        Goof    Goof    Goof

## Further Verses for "America the Beautiful"

O beautiful for the catalpa flower
And sunflowers in the field
Monarchs on the milkweed pods
To mark the bounty's yield
      America!  America!
Come sing your song of grace
For every hue beneath the blue
And every creed and race

O beautiful for prosperity
That reaches every land
And water pure cascading free
And healthcare in every hand
      O Bountiful America!
Be glad of Eternity
And may your Dream stand in the Stream
Across the Galaxy!

O beautiful for the airplane ride
That sails above the plains
And over mountains, farmlands glide
And deserts bloomed with rains!
      America!  America!
God bless thy Great Largess
And every town find full renown
And every wilderness!

O beautiful for the inventiveness
That purrs near electric streets
And freedom of the voice and press
The Dawn of Sharing greets
      America!  America!
May you build sanctity
And see your Dream stand in the Stream
      For all Eternity

O beautiful for towering ships
That speed the Milky Way
May peace imbue those starry trips
Where peaceful humans play
    America! America!
Let justice forge your stay
And spread no harm nor foes alarm
Across the Spiralling Bay!

O beautiful for an end to war
An end to class and strife
Bring Freedom Rides where no one hides
The truth in every life!
    America! America!
Come sing your song of grace
For every hue beneath the blue
And every creed and race!

    —written for Tuli Kupferberg's
    Parasong project

# I Send My Eyes Out

I send my
eyes out

for a beautiful America
and the stunning glimmer of Gaia

## COFFEE HOUSE PRESS

THE COFFEE HOUSES of seventeenth-century England were places of fellowship where ideas could be freely exchanged. In the cafés of Paris in the early years of the twentieth century, the surrealist, cubist, and dada art movements began. The coffee houses of 1950s America provided refuge and tremendous literary energy. Today, coffee house culture abounds at corner shops and online.

Coffee House Press continues these rich traditions. We envision all our authors and all our readers—be they in their living room chairs, at the beach, or in their beds—joining us around an ever-expandable table, drinking coffee and telling tales. And in the process of this exchange of stories by writers who speak from many communities and cultures, the American mosaic becomes reinvented, and reinvigorated.

We invite you to join us in our effort to welcome new readers to our table, and to the tales told in the pages of Coffee House Press books.

Please visit www.coffeehousepress.org
for more information.

# COLOPHON

*Let's Not Keep Fighting the Trojan War* was designed at Coffee House Press, in the historic Grain Belt Brewery's Bottling House near downtown Minneapolis. The text is set in Sabon.

## FUNDER ACKNOWLEDGMENTS

Coffee House Press is an independent nonprofit literary publisher. Our books are made possible through the generous support of grants and gifts from many foundations, corporate giving programs, state and federal support, and through donations from individuals who believe in the transformational power of literature. Coffee House receives major general operating support from the McKnight Foundation, the Bush Foundation, from Target, and from the Minnesota State Arts Board, through an appropriation by the Minnesota State Legislature and from the National Endowment for the Arts. Coffee House also receives support from: three anonymous donors; Abraham Associates; the Elmer L. and Eleanor J. Andersen Foundation; Allan Appel; Bill Berkson; the James L. and Nancy J. Bildner Foundation; the Patrick and Aimee Butler Family Foundation; the Buuck Family Foundation; the law firm of Fredrikson & Byron, PA.; Jennifer Haugh; Anselm Hollo and Jane Dalrymple-Hollo; Jeffrey Hom; Stephen and Isabel Keating; Robert and Margaret Kinney; the Kenneth Koch Literary Estate; Allan & Cinda Kornblum; Seymour Kornblum and Gerry Lauter; the Lenfestey Family Foundation; Ethan J. Litman; Mary McDermid; Rebecca Rand; Debby Reynolds; the law firm of Schwegman, Lundberg, Woessner, PA.; Charles Steffey and Suzannah Martin; John Sjoberg; Jeffrey Sugerman; Stu Wilson and Mel Barker; the Archie D. & Bertha H. Walker Foundation; the Woessner Freeman Family Foundation; and many other generous individual donors.

NATIONAL ENDOWMENT FOR THE ARTS

*This activity is made possible in part by a grant from the Minnesota State Arts Board, through an appropriation by the Minnesota State Legislature and a grant from the National Endowment for the Arts.* MINNESOTA STATE ARTS BOARD

TARGET.

To you and our many readers across the country, we send our thanks for your continuing support.

*Good books are brewing at coffeehousepress.org*